TRW 1901-2001
A Tradition of Innovation

Timothy C. Jacobson

WIPF & STOCK · Eugene, Oregon

Resource Publications
A division of Wipf and Stock Publishers
199 W 8th Ave, Suite 3
Eugene, OR 97401

TRW 1901-2001
A Tradition of Innovation
By Jacobson, Timothy C.
Copyright©2001 Northrop Grumman Corporation
ISBN 13: 978-1-5326-0036-4
Publication date 10/19/2016
Previously published by Northrop Grumman Corporation, 2001

TRW 1901-2001
A Tradition of Innovation

4	Preface
6	Chapter one: Hard work and good fortune
30	Chapter two: Sound strategy under siege
48	Chapter three: Stepping up and out
70	Chapter four: Two to one, to one too many
92	Chapter five: Refit and reward
110	Chapter six: Adding up and building out
124	Index

1901–2001

A Tradition of Innovation

Consider a photograph taken in 1908 or 1909. The place is Cleveland, Ohio; the subject, the welding department of what was then known as the Cleveland Cap Screw Company. Factories don't look like this anymore. A bedlam of belts and pulleys streamed down from a high ceiling onto the shop floor. There, closely packed old-fashioned machine tools ground out the goods, fashioned from tough metals and made to last. Workmen (they were all men then) tended their machines without benefit of much protective gear. Most of them donned cloth caps and heavy aprons in the simple working-class style of the times.

Compare this with an image from a recent TRW annual report. The cloth caps of the old-time workmen have made way for the white lab coats of today's technology-sophisticated knowledge workers. Gone is the heavy-machinery grit, the old industrial revolution feel of earlier times. Today's themes are global growth and integration through an array of advanced-technology products and services. The photograph captures a clean, cool, computer-assisted work environment where women are nearly as numerous as men.

Between yesterday's belts and pulleys and today's computer-assisted-design screens (or, as the wonderful acronym has it, "CAD") stretches the history of TRW as told in this short book. It passes necessarily over many names, dates, and events and tells instead a representative story about how the old picture was transformed into the new one. Both pictures belong to a continuing business success story in which financial capital, human talent, and technology, when harnessed together, serve markets and create wealth. Some of those markets today are the same markets the company served decades ago, though grown much larger. Others, like the markets in aerospace, were then still the stuff of science fiction.

Throughout the story, we find much that is foreign and much that is familiar. Throughout, we are reminded how much our predecessors have to teach us and how much we still must learn for ourselves.

Belts, pulleys, and a man's muscles were at the heart of manufacturing in TRW's earliest days. In this 1908 shop scene, workers place heads on valves and bolts. At the time, hiring was handled by a foreman who stepped out to the gate in the morning, looked over the jobseekers, and made choices to fill vacancies for the day.

Inset: At the turn of the twentieth century, few women risked the disapproval of their families for a position with a manufacturing plant. Oil-laden aprons and dirt-covered floors, however, have given way to white lab coats and sterile workplaces. This employee of TRW's space and defense business inspects a satellite antenna and is part of a workforce that today is nearly one-third female.

Record of Proceedings of the [Stockholders & Directors] Incorpora...

These Articles of Incorporation
of
The Cleveland Cap Screw Company

Witnesseth, That we, the undersigned, all of whom are citizens of the State of Ohio, desiring to form a corporation for pro[fit] under the general corporation laws of said State of Ohio...

The name of said corporation [is The Cleveland Cap Scre]w Company.

Said corporation is to be [located] in Cuyahoga County, Ohio, [where its principal business is to be trans]acted.

Said corporation is formed [for the] manufacture and sale of cap screws, machinery, tools, and any and all products manufactured from iron, steel and other metals.

Fourth. The capital stock of said corporation shall b[e] Two Hundred and Fifty Thousand Dollars ($250,000) div[ided] into Twenty-five Hundred (2500) shares of One Hundr[ed] Dollars ($100) each.

In Witness Whereof, We have hereunto set our hands, thi[s] twenty-eighth day of December, A.D. 1900

D. J. Kurtz
F. E. Bright
H. V. Bright
J. E. Morley
W. F. Carr

Cap screw advertising

The Cleveland Cap Screw Company, Cleveland, Ohio.

THE CLEVELAND CAP SCREW COMPANY, CLEVELAND, OHIO.
UNITED STATES STANDARD
HEXAGON HEAD
CAP SCREWS.
LIST

RECOGNIZE the utility of a common standard for Hexagon Head Cap Screws and Hexagon Nuts.
THE UNITED STATES STANDARD Head, as recommended by the Franklin Institute, is the accepted standard.
IF YOU BUY Nuts, they always conform to that standard.
YOU HAVE WRENCHES for these nuts; you don't want other wrenches for your cap screw heads.
LARGE BEARING SURFACE under head affords better distribution of pressure, permits use of cored holes, saves drilling, dispenses with washers.
IN FACT, the U. S. S. head is more desirable in all classes of work than the ordinary cap screw head and looks better.
YOU USE the U. S. S. head, or would like to.
YOU MAKE THEM yourselves, perhaps,—but would like to buy them.
OUR SPECIALTY is Cap Screws with U. S. S. heads of all sizes and lengths.
WE CAN FURNISH THEM with U. S. S. or V. Threads on short notice.
WE CLAIM to make a better screw, both in workmanship and material, than you have ever used.
WE CAN MAKE long finished screws or bolts cheaper than any other manufacturer.
WRITE FOR DISCOUNTS on accompanying list

1900–1929

1

Hard work and good fortune

Above: Purchased from the Grant Ball Company in the spring of 1901, the factory at 66 Clarkwood Road in Cleveland was affectionately known as the "Little Brown Hen" and served as company headquarters until 1941. The building has since been demolished, but TRW operated a piston plant at the site for many years before selling the business in 1998.

Facing page: A small band of investors signed Articles of Incorporation for the Cleveland Cap Screw Company on December 29, 1900. Books were formally opened on January 2, 1901, in a small office in downtown Cleveland.

Inset: An early product sheet doubled as promotional literature. According to records, the company was organized for the purpose of manufacturing screw machine products, including "hexagon and square head cap screws of superior quality, irregular and large heads, a specialty fillister screw, and coupling bolts and studs."

For a successful company that today thinks of itself as a veritable "house of technology," TRW's earliest history reveals an important irony. The bit of technology that got everything started had to do with a new means for manufacturing cap screws in standardized sizes and at lower cost than was possible by traditional methods. Those methods depended basically on milling down a single metal bar to the shape of a cap screw. Unfortunately, the process required more skilled labor and created more scrap metal than the market for cap screws could support. As one contemporary observer complained, the costs were "out of all proportion to the value of the finished product." The entrepreneurial founders of the Cleveland Cap Screw Company, which was established in December 1900 — by David J. Kurtz, H. Verner Bright, Frederick E. Bright, John E. Morley, and William F. Carr — thought they perceived in this difficulty a business opportunity.

Their thinking was driven by technology and dominated by 38-year-old Kurtz, one-time hardware and industrial supplies salesman with a mechanical bent. The innovation that Kurtz and company sought to bring to the mundane problem of making standardized cap screws was then newly available automatic welding equipment, manufactured by Thomson Electric Welding Company of Lynn, Massachusetts. The process of electric resistance welding, which Thomson had well protected with patents, applied high-amperage electrical current to the surfaces of pieces of metal to be joined together under pressure. The strong, smooth welds represented a marked improvement over anything that past techniques could offer and, because the process proved amenable to automation, promised to reduce the cost even as it raised the quality. Three days before Christmas 1900, Thomson licensed its patents to Kurtz, Samuel M. Mathews (an associate of Kurtz), and Frederick Bright, who also arranged to purchase the machinery needed to make two-piece cap screws. They also managed to purchase a three-year-old two-story brick factory building at 66–72 Clarkwood Road in Cleveland, and it was there that production commenced in the late summer or early autumn of 1901.

Winton automobile

Alexander Winton, left, who founded the Winton Motor Carriage Company in 1897, purchased stock in the Cleveland Cap Screw Company in 1903. Two years later he acquired controlling interest and launched the company into the promising market of automobile engine valves, right. Winton piloted one of his first vehicles on an arduous cross-country road trip in 1901.

Some employees doubted the industry's potential. An early company publication recorded a machinist's opinion: "This country's in a hell of a shape, and it'll never get any better till they get rid of the damned automobile."

From a purely technical perspective, success came quickly to the new venture. In 1905 the Franklin Institute recognized the young Cleveland company for an innovative product that was "a great gain in both economy and strength" over older methods. The trouble was that customers recognized it hardly at all, and the founders soon found themselves in the distressed position of entrepreneurs with a smart product but small demand. It soon became clear that the price of perfecting their manufacturing process and, most important, of developing their market far exceeded the group's capital resources.

Lunatic in the basement

TRW's history demonstrates the enormous influence of key individuals and fortuitous timing. Alexander Winton, though today chiefly remembered by business historians, in the first decade of the century was a more storied entrepreneur by far than even Henry Ford. He was also, as it turned out, the key link between Cleveland Cap Screw's technically superb but slow-selling cap screws and an immense new market. A Scottish immigrant, Winton was an early believer in the future of the gasoline-powered vehicle. In the early 1890s his noisy and smelly basement experiments with engines prompted his East Side Cleveland neighbors to complain to the police about the "lunatic who is making our lives miserable." But Winton was on his way up.

In 1897 he established the Winton Motor Carriage Company, which soon became, by the standards of the still-fledgling automobile industry, a considerable operation producing by 1903 more than 800 cars annually and boasting the largest automobile factory in the United States. Aimed at affluent buyers, a Winton was not a Ford.

But like Ford's company a few years later, Winton's company was responsible for significant technical innovations and pioneered in the use of interchangeable standardized parts.

Winton himself was also a great promoter of his passion for cars through racing. Barney Oldfield usually drove a Winton, and it was a Winton, traveling at a breathtaking 58 miles per hour, that captured the world automobile speed record in 1901.

Winton's attraction to Cleveland Cap Screw probably came about through his own familiarity with gasoline engine technology and its many shortcomings and perhaps because

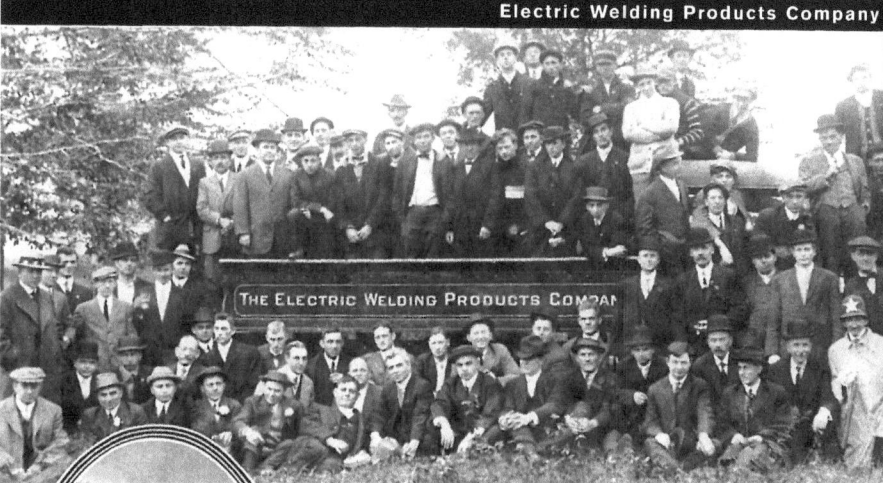

Employees of the Electric Welding Products Company posed for a group photograph after a clambake in 1913. Baseball, bowling, and theater parties were popular after-hour activities — but were not open to women.

Winton, whose Cleveland home was not far from David Kurtz's, may well have gotten to know firsthand something about the small firm's frustrating performance but intriguing prospects. What matters is this: In August 1903 Kurtz sold Winton $20,000 worth of his own stock in Cleveland Cap Screw; and then, after two years of struggle, Winton and his partners acquired the shares of the Brights and other smaller shareholders and took control of the company. Doing so accomplished not just a change in ownership and management (and name, which became Electric Welding Products Company), but also a breakthrough strategic reorientation of the young enterprise. For the new owners' intention was to make a business out of a technology by applying the process of making cap screws to the highly promising market for automobile engine valves.

Peeping Tom at the club

The mushroom-like shapes of a cap screw and those of a gasoline engine poppet valve are, after all, very much the same. The similarity had not been noticed by Alexander Winton alone. In 1904 an erstwhile telephone lineman-turned-welder for Cleveland Cap Screw Company, named Charles E. Thompson, began tinkering with automobiles. He had been hired to help install the welding equipment purchased from Thomson Electric Welding, but as Thompson's future proved, he brought to that lowly job an ambition and talent that far surpassed it. "Charlie" or "C.E.," as he would become known in the lore of the company, thought big, even at the beginning. There is a story that recounts how, in his days climbing telephone poles, he once found himself perched outside a second story window of Cleveland's posh Union Club — an exterior vantage that did not suit him at all. Engine valves, he figured, were as good a ticket as any to the inside.

Nothing is certain in business, but the intensity of Thompson's drive to succeed in it proved almost irresistible as Electric Welding Products Company turned to a fresh future. "The same large head, the same small stem, and the same great strength were all required for the valve, as they were for the standard cap screw" summarized Thompson's vision of what needed to be done. Getting started required renegotiating the license with Thomson Electric Welding to extend the use of resistance welding from cap screws to "valve stems used in engines." This Thompson accomplished early in 1906. Winton meanwhile preferred to concentrate day-to-day attention on his own car-building business, and he proved for Thompson to be the best of owners. He wasn't around much and left the running of things to Thompson, who became general manager of the refocused firm at just the moment when real success beckoned.

Eavesdropping on Cleveland's owner class taking ease at the Union Club, Charlie Thompson had learned the meaning of envy. Much of his energy thenceforth in life went toward satisfying it. Money and the pleasures it could buy mattered a great deal to Thompson. And starting from when he became general manager at $1,800 a year, Electric Welding Products Company, which became Steel Products Company, which became Thompson Products, Inc., made for Thompson a great deal of money. Through the 1910s, the company appeared to have hit the jackpot. More and more workers found good jobs in that clattering factory. Sales and profits soared. The owners rewarded themselves with princely dividends.

Success sprang from Thompson's ability to connect a technologically superior product with an exploding customer base. The product was the two-piece electrically welded poppet valve (nee cap screw). The customer base was America's youthful automobile industry, which grew phenomenally in the first two decades of the twentieth century from an annual production of about 11,000 units in 1903 to 1.5 million in 1916. America's, and then the world's, love affair with cars changed the world and changed the little business in Cleveland that made engine valves. Thompson's skill, like the success of the company he led, was two-fold. He had a simple goal, which was, as he liked to say, to engineer and manufacture automobile valves of such high quality and low cost that the automakers would not make valves themselves. And he assembled the talent needed to reach that goal. Under Thompson's early leadership, the company's first effective management team emerged. Of course, no one then talked deliberately about "teams" or even much about "management," but there is no doubt that the men who ran the company did in fact manage it very effectively and did so in concert.

Charles E. Thompson

Charles E. Thompson joined the Cleveland Cap Screw Company in 1905 and served as its president from 1915–1933. Producing automobile valves helped the infant company's fortunes soar, making it the world's leading valve manufacturer.

Facing page: Inside the "Little Brown Hen," making valves was a six-day, 79-hour-a-week job in the early 1900s, and skilled employees commanded a wage of 12.5 cents an hour. Their workdays often stretched from 6:30 a.m. until 9:15 p.m. and included short breaks with meals taken at their machines.

The Union Club

There is a story that recounts how, in his days as a telephone line repairman, Charlie Thompson found himself perched outside Cleveland's posh Union Club, left. The exterior vantage did not suit him at all, and making engine valves, he figured, was one way of getting inside to join the city's industrial elite.

Joining Thompson at the helm of the Electric Welding Products Company were J. Albert "Pete" Krider and William "Billy" D. Bartlett. The three formed the company's first effective management team, with Bartlett running the Clarkwood Road plant and Krider selling what Bartlett made.

William "Billy" D. Bartlett ran the factory on Clarkwood Road at a time when this was still possible for a man without extensive business or technical education but who was well endowed with common sense about people and had the knack of a great self-taught machinist. The sort of fellow whose work was his life and who could as likely as not be found in the factory in the middle of the night as the middle of the morning, Bartlett brought

J. Albert Krider

William D. Bartlett

a level of engineering sophistication to the process of valve manufacturing that was ahead of its time — and ahead of the competition. J. Albert "Pete" Krider sold what Bartlett made. He was a quiet man trained as a bookkeeper and with a good head for money. But he also had a sense about the place where money and goods are exchanged: the market. Together with Thompson, Krider assiduously cultivated close ties with the country's largest automakers. It was this relationship, when coupled with the reliability and appealing price of its valves, that gave the company 90 percent of the market for automotive valves by the time the United States entered World War I in 1917.

The team of Thompson, Bartlett, and Krider was broken up only by the deaths of Thompson and Bartlett in the early 1930s. In the judgment of later company head Fred Crawford, it was a team in every sense. "Not one of them would have succeeded alone," he remembered. "The three of them so completely supported each other and complemented each other that they were a success. Whenever they were busted, Krider could dig up a little more money. When Charlie took an order that was hard to make, Billy could make it." Together they understood and mastered the entire business. They modified the Thomson welding process to fit their particular needs and methodically patented the results.

As its technological prowess developed, Winton and Thompson's company found itself positioned to profit both from the rapid growth of the automobile industry and from the increasingly complex nature of cars themselves. Hundreds of different parts demanded standardization, interchangeability, and focused engineering wherewithal, as well as economies of scale in manufacture that no manufacturer — and there were more than 200 companies producing cars in America by 1910, many of them vastly undercapitalized and technology poor — could ever hope to master on its own. This fact opened wide the door to the appearance of a key new player in the industry, the independent supplier, with whom Electric Welding Products Company took an early and, in valves, a commanding position.

The automobile industry

By 1908 Henry Ford had begun mass-producing his famous Model T cars, and General Motors was organized. Charlie Thompson was busy as well, serving as a star salesman for the Electric Welding Products Company, with responsibility for calling on the automobile manufacturers in Michigan.

World War I

Reorganized in 1915 with Thompson as president, the newly renamed Steel Products Company was the nation's leading valve manufacturer and became flooded with orders during World War I. The unprecedented business spurred the company's first major expansion at the Clarkwood Road plant, pushing employment to 1,800. A parade along downtown Cleveland streets boosted patriotism and underscored the need to support the war effort.

Smart start

Looking back many years later, Fred Crawford characterized Charlie Thompson as an aggressive extrovert and a natural salesman. He also thought Thompson an opportunist and keen self-promoter. Thompson wanted to be top man, and he was impatient. In 1910, along with Bartlett and Krider and using surplus funds from Electric Welding Products, he acquired control of two small welding companies in Detroit that in turn gave him the means to get control of the Cleveland enterprise from Winton's investor group. He achieved this in 1915, when Winton accepted his offer of just over half a million dollars in cash for a majority holding.

Charlie Thompson ran the company (after 1915, Steel Products and then, after 1926, Thompson Products) as president from 1915 until his death in 1933. Ever the entrepreneurial salesman, he stamped Steel Products with a potent brand of leadership that his successors, though men of vastly differing temperaments, carried on in their own turn. One of Thompson's most positive attributes was his ability to recognize talent in others; and as the company grew in size, the resourcefulness and adaptability of its personnel set a pattern well suited to a business where just about the only constant was technological change.

On those first years under Thompson's tutelage the leaders of TRW today might well gaze back with longing. The happy beneficiary of America's then fresh love affair with the automobile, Steel Products found its valves and steering components in steadily increasing demand by scores of car manufacturers. Competitors were small garages and machine shops with, at most, regional reach. Patents guarded key manufacturing processes and helped keep competitors at bay. The resulting dominion over a vigorous, growing marketplace yielded monopoly-like profits.

The excitement that came with technological innovation in this particular new industry was not immune to the boom-and-bust cycles of the American industrial economy. The United States prospered enormously during World War I, its gross national product doubling between 1916 and 1920 and its production of automobiles rising more than 40 percent to 2.2 million vehicles. But then, during 1920 and 1921, the country tumbled into deep recession, taking the young automobile industry, and Steel Products Company, with it. Big car companies struggled: Ford slashed prices 20 percent and halted all production for six weeks; General Motors flirted with bankruptcy. Smaller companies failed wholesale, so that by mid-decade the field of carmakers shriveled to 50, a foreboding fact for companies like Steel Products that lived by supplying them.

Valve wars

The products that Steel Products supplied changed as fast as the larger economy. The technology of engine performance and valve design advanced radically during World War I to the point where Steel Products' patents on the manufacturing process for two-piece welded valves soon lost much of their value. That was because more powerful high-performance engines for cars and aircraft demanded the use of metals that could stand up to increasingly hostile environments. Unfortunately for Steel Products, the new steel alloys that met the test also resisted the process of electric resistance welding. The lesson that overreliance on patent protection can invite obsolescence hit home hard when a sharp competitor, Rich Tool Company of Chicago, pioneered a successful one-piece forged exhaust valve from an alloy of tungsten and steel. Thompson's firm soon had no choice but to take up forged valves too.

Manufacturing intensified during World War I, and workers stored valves in bulky holders they nicknamed "Christmas trees."

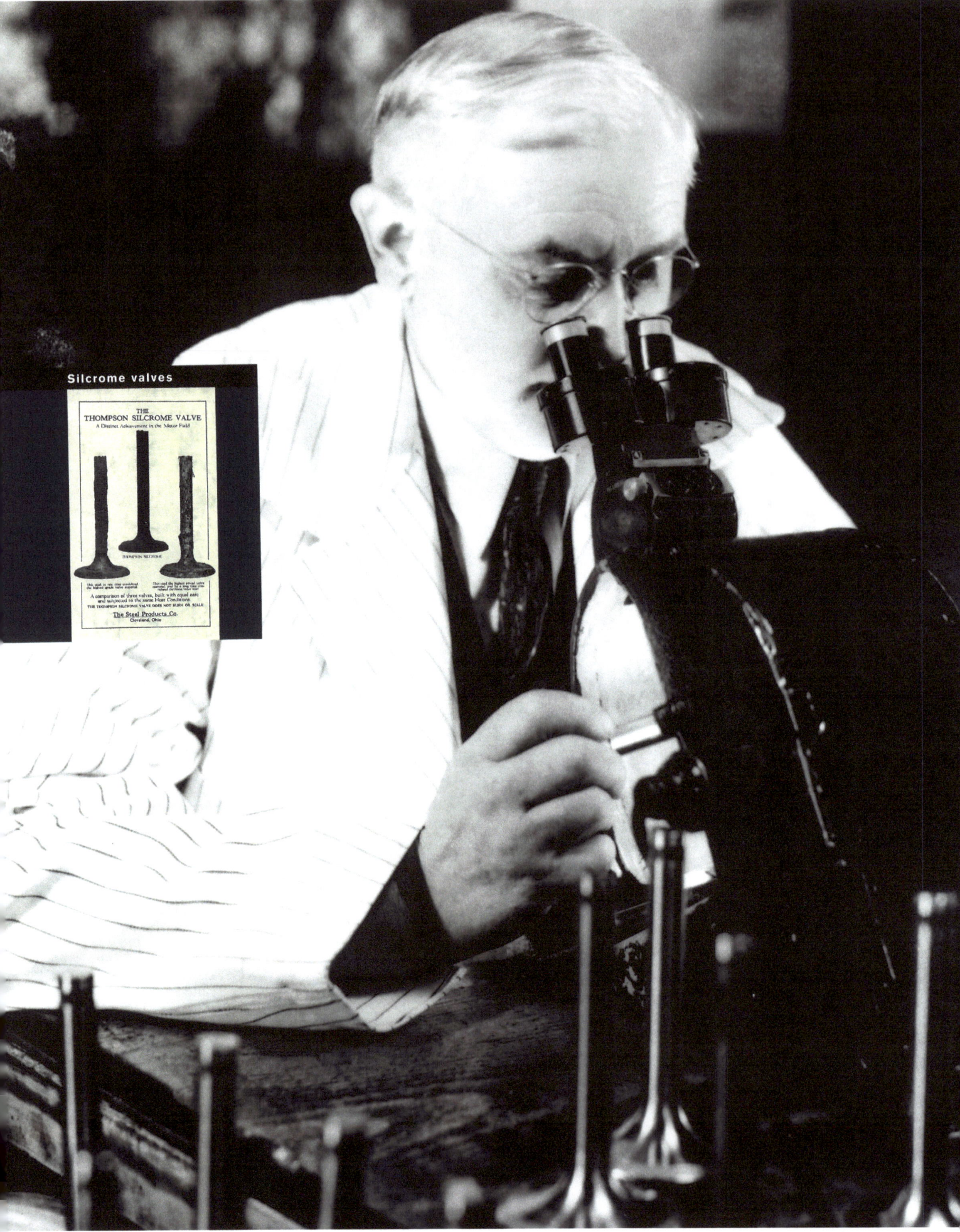
Silcrome valves

During the war, the French military equipped its Spad fighter planes with solid-forged tungsten steel valves from both Steel Products and Rich Tool. Powered by water-cooled Hispano-Suiza V8 engines, the Spad was the high-technology aircraft of its day and soon was matched by the budding aircraft of other countries. In America, the fledgling Army air service looked to a water-cooled L-12 Liberty engine. All of the new aircraft engines

French Spad fighter plane

presented suppliers with unprecedented and ever-rising technical challenges in materials and craftsmanship, and by the end of the war Steel Products was gaining experience working with all stainless steel alloys that resisted burning better than tungsten ones. In 1919 the company hired its first trained metallurgist, Dick Bissell, and began in earnest to look for the technology that would secure its position in the 1920s, as electric welding had secured it in the 1910s.

The answer that it found — a new alloy of silicon, chromium, and carbon steel — ranks high in the early technology honor roll of the company that would become TRW. The metal, which was extremely durable but also hard to work with, was actually developed at the Ludlum Steel Company, where its metallurgist, Percival Armstrong, applied for patents in 1919 and at the same time offered the technology to auto and aircraft engine builders as well as independent valve suppliers. Rich Tool hesitated, but Steel Products agreed at least to experiment with the new metal. Silcrome, as the new material came to be known, soon proved vastly superior to anything on the market. In endurance tests conducted by the U.S. Bureau of Aeronautics in 1922, tungsten-steel valves burned out after 10 hours, and chromium steel after 30 hours. Steel Products' silcrome valves still were found in good condition after nearly 400 hours of running.

Not only did Steel Products emerge from the test with a handsome order for silcrome valves from Wright Aeronautical, but a major automobile manufacturer followed up with a test of its own, aiming to drive silcrome valve-equipped cars around the clock for the then awesome distance of 25,000 miles. Again, the valves performed far beyond the specifications. It was good that they did because Steel Products in 1922 needed a success. Recession and competition had taken their toll on company morale and performance. Still, the decision to embrace the new technology was not easy. Bissell, the metallurgist, worried over the difficulties of working with the new metal, and boss Thompson himself sat on the fence. That he got off it was thanks to the persuasion of the man who would leave an even greater mark on Steel Products and its successor companies than Thompson himself.

College boy

Charlie Thompson never went to college. Fred Crawford was a Harvard man. Thompson's resentment of that fact no doubt charged their first meeting, in Cleveland in 1916. Crawford needed a job, and his lack of any particular qualification for a job at Steel Products irked Thompson. Crawford was 25 and had spent his first two years out of Harvard as a traveling tutor for other well-to-do college-bound young men. A dinner party conversation put him on the unlikely trail of Steel Products and an

Facing page: As the horsepower and speed of automobile engines increased, valves that once were satisfactory began to warp, break, and burn. In response, the company set up its first engineering laboratory, making the manufacture of valves a science.

Inset: In 1921 the Steel Products Company introduced the revolutionary Thompson silcrome valve, which offered 100 times the life of competitor valves. Machinists found the new alloy so difficult to work with that they called it the "devil's steel."

Left: The first Thompson aircraft valve equipped the Hispano-Suiza V-8 engine that powered the famous French Spad fighter in 1915, making France the company's first aviation customer. Meeting tolerances for the plane's solid-forged tungsten steel valves presented problems for some of the workmen, who were accustomed to the relatively crude methods of valve-making in the previous decade.

Frederick Coolidge Crawford joined the company as a millwright's helper in 1916. In the Harvard-educated Crawford, Thompson found a protégé whose vision of the company matched his own, but whose management talents far exceeded his own.

interview with Thompson, who was not impressed. "We can't use you," he snorted. "We don't want any college loafers around this place. We're self-made men."

So, it turned out, would be Fred Crawford. For whatever he had learned at Harvard, his greater education lay in the work that lay before him in business. Resentful as he was of Crawford's privileged background, Thompson never begrudged real talent. He offered the young college man a lowly beginning post as millwright's helper. An image (and indeed an artifact) survives from this episode that is a part of the lore of TRW. As he sensed the interview might be going nowhere, and hoping somehow to keep Thompson talking, Crawford complimented the president on a handsome inkwell he kept on his desk. Thompson seized the moment: "You like it? Well, when you get to be general manager here, I'll give it to you."

Whether or not Thompson was teasing then, he became serious enough as time passed and Crawford performed. When indeed Crawford became general manager, it was receipt of the president's inkwell from Thompson's hands that sealed his promotion. In between those two encounters, Crawford learned the business from the ground up, and he learned fast. In Crawford, Thompson had found a protégé whose vision of the company's future matched his own, but whose management talents far exceeded his own. Thompson knew what he himself wanted out of the business, which was money. He probably also knew that his desire ultimately weakened his firm. But to his credit, Thompson put in position someone equipped to save the firm from his own weaknesses. That man was Crawford.

Stories about Fred Crawford at Steel Products, then at Thompson Products, and then at TRW are legendary. He was, without a doubt, patriarch of the firm, and his legacy lives on more than 40 years after he retired as chairman in 1958. From 1916 until then, Crawford merged his life with the firm's, investing it with his own powerful convictions about the nature of business enterprise and human relations. He liked to talk about the "Triangle of Plenty" to illustrate how economic wealth was created by serving the interests of customers, investors, and employees and how increased production was the key to prosperity. Henry Ford was his particular hero.

Like Ford, Crawford wrote the pages of his own business bible as he went. In his first management job in the summer of 1922, he was dispatched to close down the company's troubled Detroit plant, but instead disobeyed orders, roused the employees to reform their ways, and rejuvenated the operation. The episode illustrated, he believed, "what happens when you stir men up, win their loyalty, make them understand what the problem is. They were fighting for their jobs." It was where he learned that "job security is the biggest worry that the worker has" and that successful management rested on successful human relations.

Cars and more cars

One Sunday afternoon during the summer of 1923, Fred Crawford visited Charlie Thompson at his country estate near Plainville, Ohio, with a singleminded aim: to convince his boss that silcrome was no flash in the pan but the surefire key to Steel Products' next surge of growth. Probably no one any less persuasive than Crawford could have succeeded, but succeed he did. Monday morning, Thompson told the whole plant that silcrome was worth whatever it might take to learn how to machine and treat it. The shop went to work and by September reported that volume manufacturing was indeed possible. Thompson then saw to licensing the Armstrong patents and getting ready for real production. It was not a moment too soon.

The president's inkwell

A famous piece of company lore, this inkwell originally was owned by Thompson. It was presented to Crawford when he became general manager in 1929 and has been passed on to each of the company's subsequent presidents.

Orders poured into Cleveland as the salesmen — who delightedly found themselves pushing a clearly superior product and at a lower price than the competition — dazzled car manufacturers with an irresistible "silcrome pitch." Dodge Brothers signed up first. Buick followed close behind. By 1925, 50 automotive manufacturers looked exclusively to Steel Products for silcrome valves.

Silcrome's success and, through it, Steel Products' stunning recapture of the engine-valve market rode the crest of the automobile boom of the 1920s. But fortune blessed Steel Products further. For not only did new cars roll off the assembly lines, but old ones also got recycled. Passenger car registration nearly tripled in those years, from 8 million to 23 million, which translated to one car for every six Americans. Keeping them running created a vast business in repair and service, along with an equally vast market for repair parts. Initially, Steel Products entered this market somewhat on the sly, being careful not to offend the automakers who wished to see their own dealers do the business.

Thompson first worked through intermediary partner firms (Ford-Clark, Parts Service, Garage Service Company), which in 1923 were consolidated, with Steel Products production manager John Kerwin in charge. The replacement parts business was organized openly as an independent subsidiary of Steel Products the following spring and took the name "Thompson Products." Crawford had to battle to convince the carmakers that it was to their advantage to let Thompson also supply the replacement business, which in reality the manufacturers, who were mainly interested in selling new vehicles, could never do themselves. Cheap, poorly manufactured parts would otherwise capture the field and threaten to take with them the makers' own good reputations, Crawford argued. His persistence paid off, and the new business prospered as the country was divided into sales territories and more reps were added, each with the goal to sign up 100 jobbers across the country, a number soon surpassed.

Airborne

U.S. President Herbert Hoover proudly held up the automobile industry as the potent symbol of the nation's prosperity and famously envisioned an America with (in addition to a chicken in every pot) two cars in every garage. Next to cars, the aircraft industry of the 1920s was a relative pygmy. But it was a pygmy to watch. Down the road of Steel Products' future, the theme of flight was destined to fill an ever larger place. The company's business fortunes were to evolve in the context of these two compelling cultural enthusiasms. Both of them — automobiles and airplanes (and later spacecraft) — put technology into the service of movement. Nothing could have fit the twentieth century better. Both of them were rich in technological possibility and demanded the utmost alertness to change. Both proved good choices on which to build a business.

The aircraft industry, like the automotive industry in the 1920s, was growing fast. Steel Products participated in that growth through its superior engine valve technology. The country turned out fewer than 1,000 planes in 1925, and just four years later, 6,000. Even then, many had more than one engine, and each engine had numerous valves. The evolution of engine design doubled the challenge for quality components. Early aircraft engines had been water-cooled, but the development, beginning in World War I, of air-cooled models that ran at extremely high temperatures and much greater compression, raised the technical bar, particularly for exhaust valves.

An engineer from England, Sam D. Heron, who was employed as a civilian with the U.S. Army Air Corps at McCook Field near

---

Thompson silcrome valves

Thompson silcrome valves were the choice for automobile manufacturers by the mid-1920s. Indeed, orders poured into Cleveland, with the Dodge Brothers signing up first, followed closely by Buick. Demand for the valve was also felt from automobile repair shops and thrust the company into the replacement business in 1924 with a line of valves, bolts, and starting cranks.

The company's name was changed to Thompson Products, Inc., in 1926 to honor its president. One year later, Thompson Products advertised that 18 of its all-new sodium-cooled valves were at the heart of Charles Lindbergh's *Spirit of St. Louis* as he crossed the Atlantic Ocean. A telegram from Wright Aeronautical, maker of the engine, called Thompson Products' role an "essential contribution" to Lindbergh's brilliant achievement.

Dayton, Ohio, was the first to hit on a solution. If an exhaust valve were designed with a hollow stem and filled with a heat-absorbing substance, then heat might be successfully drawn away from the valve head and into, as he put it, the "cocktail shaker" of the surrounding stem. Heron experimented with both metallic salts and sodium alloys and received patents in the middle 1920s. While competitor Rich Steel Products in Detroit commercialized the product first, Thompson's company licensed Heron's patents and soon excelled at the complex technical challenge of manufacturing hollow-stemmed valves filled with volatile metallic sodium.

Its success was thanks in large part to Lee Clegg, a highly effective and hardworking technical sales representative who liked to work on big customers in the comfort of his hunting lodge in Gatineau, Quebec. Clegg was an affable salesman, but one who always chose his words "with the care of an engineer working on blueprints." His grasp of valve technology helped establish winning relationships with key engine manufacturers determined to move quickly into modern radial air-cooled designs. Wright Aeronautical and Pratt & Whitney both used Thompson Products valves, which in 1927 found their way into the engine that kept aloft the most

famous aircraft of the era. To power the attempt at flying the Atlantic nonstop, the J-5 Wright Whirlwind engine that went into Charles Lindbergh's *Spirit of St. Louis* at first was planned for the use of Rich Steel valves. But when engineers raised questions about the J-5's ability to run continuously for the required 40 hours, Thompson Products sales engineers were ready with the alternative of still-experimental Thompson sodium-cooled valves. Lindbergh himself agreed to the change; and as a consequence 18 of the new valves, made in Cleveland, crossed the Atlantic to Paris with the soon-to-be-legendary young aviator. Charlie Thompson, coincidentally just then on one of his many pleasure trips to France, was part of the excited throng that welcomed the little single-engine plane when it set down safely at Le Bourget airport on May 21.

Lindbergh, and Thompson Products' sodium-cooled valves, logged more than 3,000 miles on that long-ago first nonstop flight across the North Atlantic. The image of the begoggled boyish flier, posed in front of his *Spirit of St. Louis*, is one that has stood up (rather like the valves) to long use in the advertising and public relations annals of the company that became TRW. It is an arresting, romantic image. In the annals of human flight, probably nothing equaled it until the landing of the first Apollo spacecraft on the surface of the moon in 1969. And that flying machine, like Lindbergh's more primitive one, could not have made the trip without TRW technology.

The power of flight on the twentieth-century imagination gave to companies that could identify themselves with it a special forward-looking character. Prosaic-sounding Thompson Products learned how to take fullest advantage of this, at first through the talents of Raymond S. Livingstone, hired as the company's first publicity manager in 1929. Livingstone was himself a pilot (and a

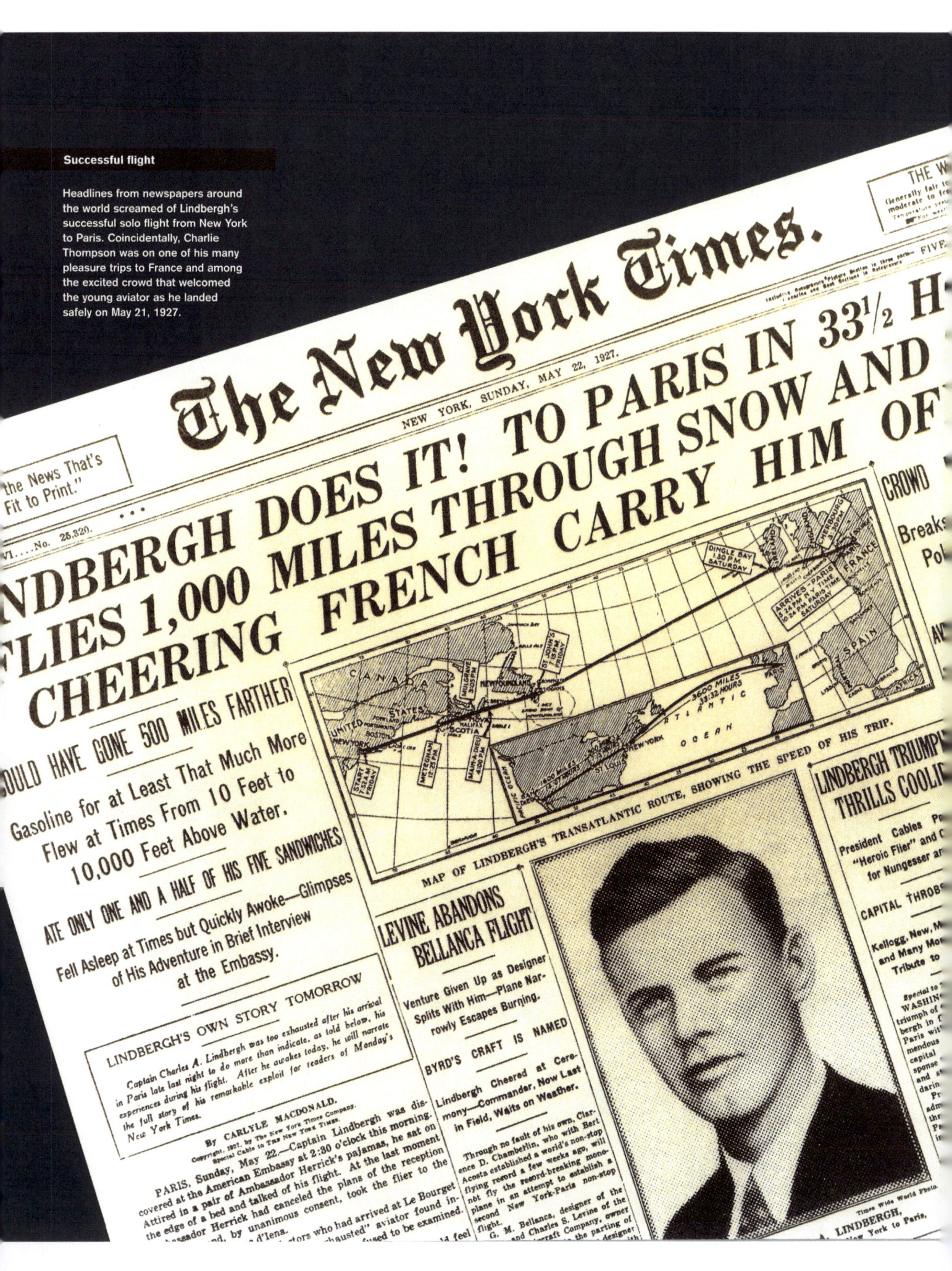

Successful flight

Headlines from newspapers around the world screamed of Lindbergh's successful solo flight from New York to Paris. Coincidentally, Charlie Thompson was on one of his many pleasure trips to France and among the excited crowd that welcomed the young aviator as he landed safely on May 21, 1927.

Thompson valves at the heart of Lindbergh's plane

Pictured with his legendary *Spirit of St. Louis*, Lindbergh himself approved the use of Thompson valves in the plane's engine rather than valves from Rich Steel, as originally planned. The decision proved a boon for Thompson Products, whose valves acquired an esteemed reputation and went on to power the motor of Sir Charles Kingford-Smith's monoplane on his 7,800-mile trip to Australia in 1928.

Right: Thompson Products participated in the 1929 National Air Races, held at Cleveland's new municipal airport, by sponsoring one event. The involvement led to the establishment in 1930 of the annual Thompson Trophy Race as well as a national competition among sculptors to design the trophy. Orville Wright was among the judges who selected the 32-inch bronze sculpture of Icarus reaching for the sun, by Clevelander Walter A. Sinz, as the winner.

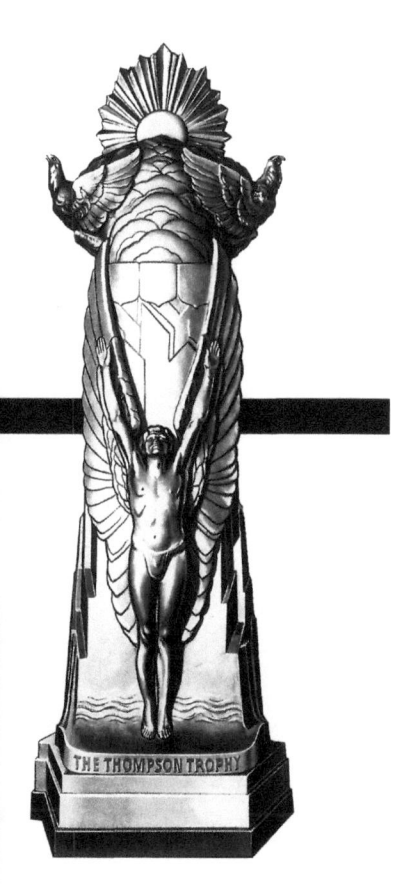

former newspaperman) who understood the thrill of aviation not just to those few who actually went aloft, but also to the millions of spectators who didn't and probably never would.

Lindbergh's had been a feat of abridging space — of going a great distance. But flight at the beginning of the 1930s more and more fascinated in its other dimension — abridging time. Speed was all. (Even in 1927, the *Spirit of St. Louis,* loaded to the hilt as it was with gasoline, was a relatively poky machine.) In 1929 Cleveland boosters convinced the National Aeronautic Association to bring the three-year-old National Air Races to the city's new municipal airport. They hired a professional promoter and assembled an irresistible package of prizes and events. They were rewarded with a show that attracted 100,000 people over 11 days of races. Then, as now, company sponsorship figured large in everyone's hopes, with 60 races looking for a flag to carry. By the time race organizers called on Thompson Products, the list, in Livingstone's estimation, had been "pretty well picked over." That fact did not keep him from seeing the opportunity. For the purposes of achieving publicity, one of the best remained available: something dubbed the "International Land Plane Free-for-All." The name meant just what it said. Anything without pontoons was welcome ("superchargers and special fuels permitted"), and the 10-lap, five-mile course around fixed pylons was tailor made for thrilling spectator viewing. The company spent $25 for the first "Thompson Trophy" and reaped a publicity bonanza for its investment. Aviator Doug Davis, flying a civilian monoplane powered by a Curtiss-Wright Whirlwind engine, won with an average speed of 191.1 mph. Davis easily left behind the closest military competitors (all still biplanes), which brought a stir among politicians and editorialists over the sorry state of the nation's military preparedness. But it was the front-page-quality electricity of Livingstone thrusting the trophy into the flyer's hands that symbolized the event and convinced Clegg and Crawford to try to make the event a perennial. There would, they decided, be a permanent Thompson Trophy, and a 30-inch-tall bronze likeness of Icarus reaching sunward was specially sculpted for it. The particular design owed much to Fred Crawford, who said he wanted something better than "just another naked lady waving a flag."

Too good to last

Thompson infused the company with his own considerable entrepreneurial instincts and communicated to the talented men he gathered around him the importance of measured risk-taking. The firm's ability to extract from the cultural enthusiasms of the age, and from Thompson's leadership, an impressive business success bespoke several concrete accomplishments. It had stayed abreast of technological change and had found markets hungry for the technologies it had to offer. It had applied its financial and human capital wisely to meet the challenge of difficult manufacturing processes. And it had begun to develop a group of managers capable of coordinating the workings of a sophisticated industrial enterprise in lines of business beset by accelerating change.

But by its fourth decade of existence, the 1930s, Thompson Products also found itself tested and under pressure both from within and without. From the inside, one of its greatest assets also turned out to be one of its gravest burdens. This was the character of Charlie Thompson himself. As president of the company and its largest shareholder, Thompson could do largely as he chose, and in general he chose rightly. He made good deals. He was a convincing salesman. He secured solid patent protection on key manufacturing processes. And he was lucky. Competition, to start, was small and disorganized.

Lowell Bayles, pilot of the fastest plane in the 1931 speed race, accepted the Thompson Trophy and a handshake from a declining Charlie Thompson, left. Two years later, Thompson suffered a heart attack and died in Washington, D.C., where he had traveled to meet with other car parts manufacturers.

In keeping with Thompson's final wishes, half of his ashes were interred, and half were scattered over downtown Cleveland from a red and yellow monoplane flown by his old friend and fabled aviator, Jimmy Doolittle.

Hubbell's first drawing of a Thompson Trophy winner

Customers were numerous and no one of them too large or powerful. Demand for everything the company made — valves and steering parts for cars and valves for airplanes — was strong and rising fast.

But even as Thompson's firm succeeded, his personal focus shifted more and more from getting to spending. It was not unusual for firms in the 1920s to pay out big dividends, for stockholders of the era commonly looked for regular cash returns from their investments rather than long-term capital gains. But in Thompson's case, the tendency was pronounced, and it had unfortunate consequences. Fred Crawford, while he admired Thompson and certainly had reason to feel in his debt, also saw the dark side and understood the threat to the enterprise they all had built. Thompson's need for cash to support extravagant personal tastes was reflected in company payouts from net income as high as 78 percent in the late 1920s. "An admirable person in many ways," Crawford allowed, but his main motivation (along with Bartlett's and Krider's) "in running the company was to take money out of it." By the late 1920s, Thompson was a millionaire several times over and married to his high-maintenance third wife, Gloria Hopkins, with whom he reveled in the life of a big spender. There were fashionable houses in Cleveland, a townhouse in New York City, a $25,000 Duesenberg automobile (when a Cadillac could be had for one-tenth that sum), and, most ostentatious of all, "Chateau Gloria," his villa at Cape Ferrat on the French Riviera, which featured, among other luxuries, a sunken swimming pool just off the second floor bathroom. One thinks of the image of a younger Thompson, the telephone lineman, looking in enviously at the "owners" at the club, and wonders if at last he was satisfied.

Probably not. But the company, Thompson Products, certainly paid a price for its namesake's personal passions. That would have been true even in a stable business and technological climate, which the 1920s for the automobile business decidedly were not. The vast scale of manufacturing and distribution challenges that confronted the rapidly growing business of building cars favored big players, and by the end of the decade 90 percent of the new-car market belonged to the Big Three: General Motors, Ford, and Chrysler. Such consolidation conditioned the growth of the supplier industry as well. It became an industry increasingly governed by standards and standard practices. Technical standardization especially spread, championed by the Society of Automotive Engineers, whose initials became part of the vocabulary of the automobile age, as anyone mundanely getting an oil change ("SAE" 10W30) can attest. Standardization meant a reduction in the number and variety of parts that suppliers had to produce, it permitted longer production

Charles H. Hubbell

The Thompson Trophy Races were featured in a series of paintings by Cleveland artist Charles Hubbell. Doug Davis, flying a Curtiss-Wright-powered commercial monoplane in 1929, was the first Thompson Trophy winner, and his plane became the subject of a Hubbell drawing.

Hubbell's work was reproduced on calendars that Thompson Products gave to its best customers and sold to the public. Sales were profitable because, like Thompson and Crawford, the country quickly was becoming enamored with the field of aviation.

THE "Flyer's Friend"
Thompson Valves

runs at lower unit costs, and it reduced suppliers' reliance on the whims of any one specific customer. But there were negatives as well. Growth of a few powerful car manufacturers altered the fundamental balance of bargaining power between the manufacturers and the companies, like Thompson Products, that supplied them. To this had to be added the danger that the big car companies, as they grew bigger and more powerful, would go into parts-making for themselves ("backward integration," as economists would say). This was a danger that proved real enough. During the 1920s, each of the Big Three carmakers manufactured a portion of the valves needed for its own vehicles, with the result that the overall proportion of purchased parts in American automobiles fell more than 50 percent between 1922 and 1926. Dependent as it was, and was destined to be, on a few key large customers, Thompson Products had but one defense. It was a defense that it learned early and practiced to perfection in the years to come. As Charlie Thompson endlessly put it, and as every company leader professed after him: "We must make our parts so good and at such low cost that the car manufacturers won't want to make their own."

For all his entrepreneurial verve and skill at bringing bright, highly motivated people into the enterprise, Thompson would not have achieved great success without great timing. Thompson Products prospered on the twin pillars of its own hard work and the good fortune to have set about its particular lines of work in the fabulous 1920s, when two of the country's most exciting industries, automobiles and aircraft, came into their own. Its success came about with the right match of internal strengths to external conditions. In the 1930s, the external conditions changed drastically and put the internal strengths severely to the test.

Women in manufacturing

Facing page: In the 1930s Thompson Products published a series of advertisements that touted the company's superior valve technology to a country that was just awakening to the possibilities of air travel. The series of "Flyer's Friend" ads appeared in such national magazines as Fortune and Life.

Above: The first women employed in any considerable number at TP took jobs as inspectors during the World War I manpower shortage. Early company publications, however, reveal that a few women were on the payroll as early as 1912, shaving valve heads and drilling holes in bolts.

1930–1939

2

Sound strategy under siege

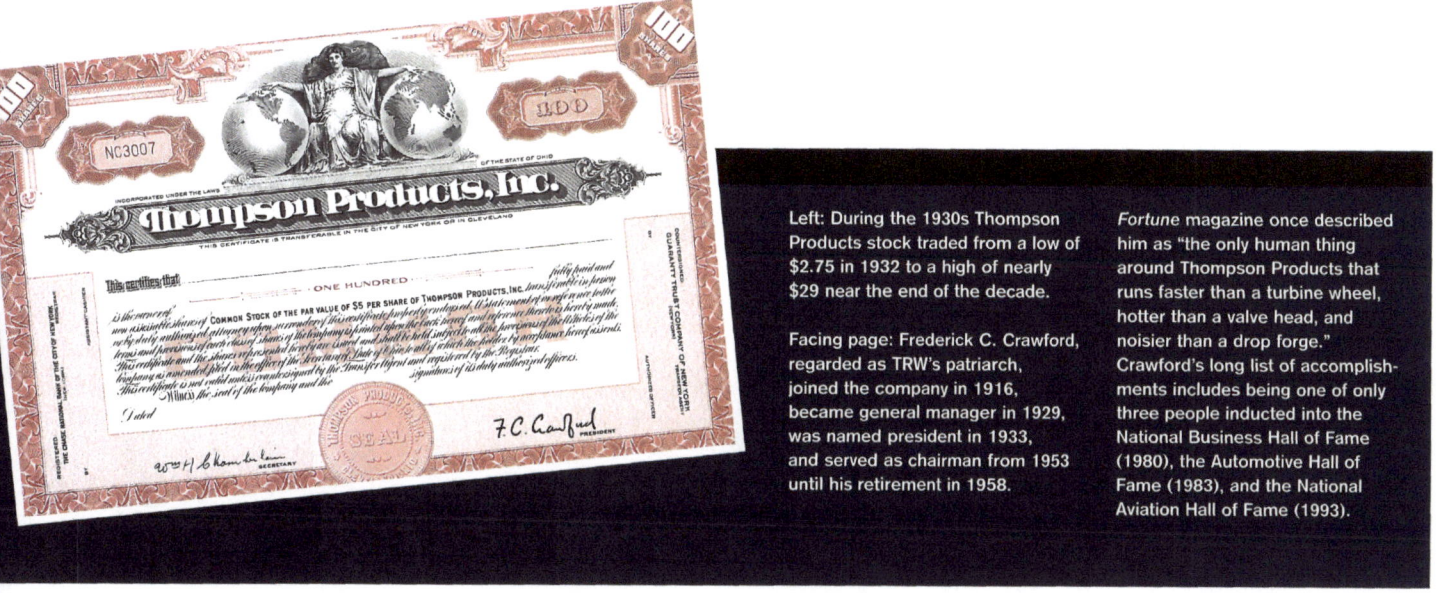

Left: During the 1930s Thompson Products stock traded from a low of $2.75 in 1932 to a high of nearly $29 near the end of the decade.

Facing page: Frederick C. Crawford, regarded as TRW's patriarch, joined the company in 1916, became general manager in 1929, was named president in 1933, and served as chairman from 1953 until his retirement in 1958.

Fortune magazine once described him as "the only human thing around Thompson Products that runs faster than a turbine wheel, hotter than a valve head, and noisier than a drop forge." Crawford's long list of accomplishments includes being one of only three people inducted into the National Business Hall of Fame (1980), the Automotive Hall of Fame (1983), and the National Aviation Hall of Fame (1993).

Fred Crawford was an inside man and an outside man. Between the time he was elected president of Thompson Products at the bottom of the Great Depression in November 1933 and the end of World War II, he took a small company and made it into a much larger one, and he made himself at the same time into a big character in American business. It was a typical Crawford feat made possible by two kinds of understanding. First was the understanding that came from attentiveness to the text of TP's chosen line of business in automotive and aircraft parts manufacturing. Second was the understanding that came from attentiveness to the context for TP's particular business in an age of embattled democratic capitalism. Crawford loved challenge, and in the circumstances bequeathed him by his predecessor and served up by the American economy and politicians in the 1930s and 1940s, he found plenty of it. Inside, the challenge was to consolidate the success that good fortune had bestowed on TP in more prosperous times and to prepare it for prosperous times once again. Outside, the challenge was to protect America's free enterprise system from government meddling and so secure the future for his firm and thousands of others that shared its values.

First-rate boss

Inside or outside, the figure of Fred Crawford commanded attention. Part of this was style, but most of it was substance. The style early became a part of the lore of TP and soon eclipsed the Thompson memory. Crawford cultivated an image of frenetic activity tempered with playfulness. He was one of those individuals blessed with small need for sleep, and consequently he got a great deal done. No sybarite like Thompson, he spent all his abundant energy on work and had the gift to make others believe it was fun.

Crawford surrounded himself with other youthful high-energy figures, and members of the team no doubt fed off one another. Arch Colwell served as head of engineering. College-trained metallurgist Harry Bubb was chief engineer. Ray Livingstone received the challenge of becoming the company's expert on personnel management. Eugene McBride, Matt Graham, and George Stauffer managed the Cleveland, Michigan, and Canadian plants. From the outside, Crawford recruited a young lawyer, Dave Wright, as his personal assistant and Tom Duggan to run the Service Division. The group's average age was 37.

Crawford kept everybody busy and entertained. But it was fun with a purpose, and the purpose was business, and business meant no fooling around. Hard times would not allow it, and the boss (who probably wasn't half as secure as he let on) knew just how close lurked the dark shadow of failure in those years. Underneath the joker, Crawford had a very hard edge. Master of plain talk and a few simple principles, he never left much room for doubt about where he stood and what he expected of those who stood around him.

"It's a goddam tough fight" was how Crawford thought of the job that TP and every other good company faced every day, just in keeping the doors open. "Business is a struggle between human wants, and the manager is the guy who has got to satisfy those wants."

The particular wants that TP had to satisfy were, as Crawford saw them, much the same as had occupied the company under Thompson: automotive parts for the original equipment and the replacement markets, and aircraft engine parts. Under Crawford, TP would do the same things it had done before, but it would do them differently. As the company weathered the Depression, Crawford focused on strategies to ensure its sound and balanced growth. He would pour resources into the search for new products. He would reexamine every inch of every manufacturing process in the search for increased efficiency. He would stretch TP's market reach through direct investment and careful acquisitions. He would gather valuable brand names in the replacement market. And he would put the most energetic managers he could find into key posts in the plants and at headquarters to make it all happen. By the end of the 1930s he would have transformed Thompson's fortunate fiefdom into a thoroughly professionalized organization with a growing reputation for technical excellence and progressive management.

Crawford's TP was managed for the long term and thus was better able by far than Thompson's TP to cope with difficulties in the short term.

Inside fixes

Years later, Crawford wisecracked that "a wonderful time to get to the top is when things couldn't get worse." Depressions dampen expectations: "If you manage to crawl out of the gutter and up onto the curb, people think you're a genius." Fred Crawford did not think himself a genius, and at the time, in the 1930s he was not sure at all that things couldn't get even worse than they already were.

Stories of Crawford's restless energy and sense of humor were legion among his friends. That same charisma appealed to employees and helped him minimize the rift that often existed between management and production workers. Crawford, in a chef's hat, never missed an opportunity to have fun and once quipped, "It's good business to create situations in which employees can have a good laugh at the boss' expense."

Expanded product line

This 1936 advertisement appeared in *Fortune* magazine and boasted of Thompson's role as the "anonymous" source for parts that made automobiles and airplanes safer and more powerful.

But timing was in fact with him. By early 1934 demand for new cars and replacement parts for old ones was rising once more. With a critical (and by later standards very modest) loan of $100,000 from National City Bank, Crawford made important capital investments in new equipment for fashioning valves and plating pistons. He also, as quickly as he could, took care of people, restoring pay cuts taken by salaried workers in 1932 and 1933 and hiring back laid-off wage-roll employees. The board even started dispensing dividends again on preferred stock, which had been suspended two years before. The investment paid off, as sales rose to $6.6 million in 1934 with earnings of almost $400,000. New products, Crawford was especially proud to report — knee-action spring sets for Chevrolet, retainer locks, valve seat inserts, water pumps — made up a hefty $800,000 share of total revenues.

Except for the recession that came near the end of the decade, the healthy trend of recovery continued unabated. Though still below 1929 levels, sales in 1937 topped $14 million, and the stock price rose to nearly $29 from a low of $2.75 five years before. While holders of common stock started once again to enjoy dividends in 1935, Crawford and the board kept the payout ratio low and jealously plowed earnings back into the business to improve products and further penetrate markets. With the last of the Thompson family interest relinquished (for a nice profit) in 1936, Crawford and his managers could look to the future undistracted.

What they saw was conditioned by their own business vision. As it turned out, that vision matched remarkably well, if not quite perfectly, what the future actually held in store. The three product lines — original equipment, replacement parts, and aircraft engine components — on which the business had come down to them looked to be reasonable supports for post-Depression Thompson Products too, but only if management stayed alert to technology and kept a sharp eye out for shifts in the marketplace. Thompson had been fortunate to have gotten things started during America's early love affair with cars and trucks. From that day to this, however, no other product could come close to the automobile both as symbol of American culture and as engine of American prosperity. The "fling" of the 1910s and the Roaring Twenties evolved into an indissoluble and highly fruitful marriage, as the industry's strong recovery even in the hard times of the 1930s foreshadowed.

At Thompson Products, there were certainly no doubters. As motor vehicle registrations roared upward again, Crawford's men scrambled to polish up the firm's historic competencies in valves. The old bread-and-butter Silcrome No. 1 made way for newer alloys that kept the metallurgists busy — Silcrome XB for cars and light trucks, Silcrome X-10 for heavy trucks, Silcrome XCR for high-performance engines. But Crawford believed even more opportunity was out there, and Colwell's development staff soon found itself purchasing a small fleet of cars for the purpose of dismantling them, piece by piece, in search of new parts for TP to manufacture. Meantime, the old challenge of finding ways to make valves last longer yielded a rotating valve device in 1938 that turned out to be better on the drawing board than in actual use, but that evolved in the 1940s into the highly successful "Thompson Rotocap."

Keeping ahead of the technology curve was essential to keeping competitors in valve manufacturing at bay, particularly the automotive manufacturers themselves, who from time to time made worrisome feints in that direction. In 1937 Crawford caught a rumor that one of his biggest accounts, Chrysler, was looking to diversify its supply or even looking for a new supplier altogether. Jadson Motor Products Company in far-off

ANONYMOUSLY YOURS,
Thompson Products Inc.

FAST, SLEEK, SAFE, the new automobiles roll out over the nation's highways... more powerful, more safe, because of unseen Thompson parts. » » »

Development of the automobile engine was at a standstill until Thompson perfected the Silcrome Valve to stand the greater heats of greater speed. » » » » »

Road safety was often in jeopardy until Thompson designed the eccentric, the rubber core and more recently the dual-bearing tie rod for independently sprung front wheels. » »

Motor performance was stepped up—and maintenance costs lowered—when Thompson brought out chrome-plated piston pins, Duracrome valve-seat inserts, and a revolutionary valve retainer. » » » » » » » »

These are typical of the many developments achieved by Thompson engineers in close cooperation with car builders. Thompson may be anonymous to many car owners, but automotive engineers know and respect this name. Practically every automobile and truck on the road or airplane in the sky uses and depends on parts in the Thompson line. » » »

« « « » » »

THOMPSON PRODUCTS, INC.
CLEVELAND · DETROIT · ST. CATHARINES, ONTARIO
Manufacturers of Motor and Chassis Parts Made to Car Builders' Specifications
Pioneers of the Thompson Silcrome Valve and of the New Silcrome-X Valve

Thompson Products

TP's Service Division

Sales to the replacement market in the 1930s by TP's Service Division soared from $2.1 million to nearly $5 million, equaling the company's sales to original equipment manufacturers. Under the effective management of Tom Duggan and Jim Syvertsen, the Service Division increased its geographical coverage as well, opening new retail outlets and warehouses each year. By 1938 TP replacement parts were sold in more than 75 countries.

California, which had a license for silcrome products, looked like the probable partner. The prospect was scary enough for Crawford to make a preemptive strike, buying Jadson for $260,000 in stock. The deal bolstered TP technologically, for Jadson's line included high-performance valves for racing cars and heavy engines (Jadson valves could be found in most of the winning cars running at Indianapolis) and for aircraft. It also enhanced TP's position in the lucrative replacement parts market and gave it its first foothold on the West Coast, where a large part of TP's (eventually TRW's) future, starting in the 1950s, would be played out.

Even without help from Jadson, TP's replacement business was already coming into its own and by the end of the decade equaled original equipment sales to car and truck manufacturers. Even though new-vehicle sales rebounded with surprising resilience in the late 1930s, the depressed economy generally saw drivers coaxing more miles out of older cars. TP correctly sensed this powerful parallel current and maneuvered smartly into it. The day-to-day job belonged to the Service Division, managed by Tom Duggan and Jim Syvertsen, who methodically applied a strategy of geographical expansion. New warehouses and retail stores mushroomed across the country, and a vigorous export department introduced TP replacement parts to more than 75 countries overseas.

In a company perhaps best known for technological prowess, Duggan and Syvertsen's success underscored the importance of marketing savvy. They bundled together commonly needed replacement parts and instructions, called them "Service Packages," and appealed to buyers looking for one-stop engine repair convenience. At the same time, they convinced Crawford to get the company name boldly out in front of its products with a national advertising program.

TP had the products, and now it built the brand. The famous Thompson Products Indian-"tepee" logo soon decorated every ad and every package, and no mechanic in the automotive business had any excuse not to know whose parts were best or not to call for them by their brand name. This was important, since from the final consumer's — the driver's — point of view, TP was by nature something of a hidden company: It made parts for other people's products. Its own products were hidden away under the hoods and inside the engines of machines known to the motoring public as "Chevys" and "Fords" and "Dodges." But as the "tepee" popped up in more and more service station and garage windows and retail outlets, the TP content of America's cars and trucks grew plainer for everyone to see. Market expansion also got a boost in 1935 with acquisition of competitor Toledo Steel Products Company (TSP). Controlled back in the early 1920s by Charlie Thompson, TSP had been brought low by the Depression, and Crawford snapped it up for just half of what it was probably worth. TSP made fine replacement valves, which it knew how to sell through a national network of more than 650 distributors. Under its new owners, TSP would be operated as a TP subsidiary and was transformed overnight from a powerful competitor to a powerful parallel brand.

Not all of TP's manufacturing and marketing know-how, however, could create demand where there was none. This was the short-term problem with the hoped-for third product leg of the company: products for the still small

The TP brand

During the 1930s the company's Service Division mounted a nationwide advertising campaign to build awareness of the TP brand. The division created a new logo — the TP tepee — that adorned its advertisements and replacement parts packages. The logo became a widely recognized symbol for quality by auto mechanics everywhere.

aviation industry. Military budgets for the army's and navy's much-neglected flying corps were minuscule, and commercial flight had not yet begun to challenge the railroads in moving Americans around their continent-sized country. It was not until 1940, in fact, with much of the world again at war and American mobilization kicking in, that the United States produced as many airplanes as it had back in 1929. A stagnant market kept TP's sales of aircraft engine valves stuck at never more than a tenth of its total revenues through the 1930s, and this was despite some impressive technological innovations that were to pay off only later. While evolution of bigger aircraft engines, and aircraft with more of them, kept the business alive even at low volumes, the business dynamic of manufacturing for the aviation industry differed fundamentally from that for cars and trucks.

Aircraft engine valves

While TP's original equipment and replacement businesses enjoyed healthy growth, the company's line of aircraft parts remained grounded. Despite impressive technological innovations, the wildly successful Thompson Trophy Races, and advertisements like this one, sales of aircraft engine valves never exceeded more than a tenth of the company's total revenues throughout the 1930s.

"Any means available to get dependable performance" was how Arch Colwell described the technology component of the business of airborne valves. With earthbound ones, it was just "working to a budget."

As they worked to their stubborn budgets, Fred Crawford's men clawed growth from a still-crippled national economy, confident that when the cycle turned their industry would rebound with the best. The trouble was, for them and for businessmen everywhere, that as the 1930s ground on the cycle did not turn, at least not decisively. It was a decade filled with diversions and distress.

Crawford coped in ways revealing of his own two-sided nature: the funny man and the serious all-business boss. The National Air Races continued in Cleveland, which, thanks largely to Crawford's lobbying, became their permanent home after 1937. Each year, the newsreels showed the ever dapper head of Thompson Products making his Labor Day presentation of the Thompson Trophy to some windblown aviator, typically with a movie star or prominent politician close at hand. Icons in their own lifetimes, Charles Lindbergh and Amelia Earhart both walked across Crawford's platform at one time or another and, along with the mustachioed Red Baron-lookalike Roscoe Turner (three-time race winner in 1934, 1938, and 1939), made for particularly rich photo opportunities.

Outside battles

To this day the 1930s define distress in America's economic vocabulary. The Depression experience left many shattered; others it strengthened. Fred Crawford was one of the latter. It strengthened him as hardship routinely does to a man who is not spoiled. But it also strengthened in him particular beliefs about business and government — and management and labor — that branded the

Roscoe Turner

Turner, resembling the Red Baron, stood in front of the silver No. 29 Turner-Laird Special that brought him Thompson Trophy wins in 1938 and 1939. He covered the 300-mile race both years with a speed that never broke 285 mph. Turner was the race's only three-time winner and, in fact, the only repeat winner. The final Thompson Trophy Race was held in 1959.

private culture of the growing TP organization and that branded TP's leader as a man sure to be heard from on some of the big public issues of his day.

Crawford was not a man to hide strong convictions, and one of his strongest was his dislike of President of the United States Franklin D. Roosevelt. Crawford was a "That Man" Republican who didn't have much use for Mrs. Roosevelt either. He loathed Franklin and Eleanor down to his boots and dedicated his formidable gifts as a communicator to refuting everything they stood for. This was, it is important to note, both the private and the public Crawford speaking as one. For it was not just that Crawford was a reverent descendant of conservative New England Yankees, but also that he was head of the Thompson Products business and had a duty — as if part of his job description — to bring to battle forces hostile to it. Roosevelt's "New Deal" represented everything known to Crawford to threaten America's free enterprise system. Roosevelt (with an upbringing hardly more radical than Crawford's), of course, saw it just the other way around, believing that it would take a genuinely "New Deal" to save capitalism from itself. But Crawford smelled less a new deal than a stacked deck, and he soon made himself into one of the "Squire of Hyde Park's" most fearsome business foes.

The New Deal, which commenced with the omnibus legislation of Roosevelt's first hundred days in office, signaled an ominous leap forward for government regulation of the economy. This took many forms, including new public agencies to monitor agriculture, the banks, securities markets, the provision of welfare, and regulation of public corporations. But most onerous to businessmen like Crawford, who had factories to run and workforces to pay and manage, was one piece of legislation in particular: the National Industrial Recovery Act, which gave birth to the National Recovery Administration, or NRA. The NRA was to attempt, through a complex system of codes, to reshape industry pricing, competitive practice, and labor relations. The act's notorious Section 7(a), which stipulated maximum hours and minimum wages, also guaranteed workers the right to organize and bargain collectively with their employers, "free from interference, coercion or restraint." This insulted Crawford and inflamed him.

It also set organized labor on the march, as national unions, particularly national industrial unions, pressed to organize workers left out of traditional craft representation and to discredit the so-called "company unions" encouraged by many employers, including TP. Reasonable shorthand for Crawford's position would be to say that he was fervently pro-labor and adamantly anti-union. He once said, much later in life, that no one should ever be awarded an MBA without having spent at least a year working on the floor in a factory. He had, as a day laborer at Steel Products back in 1916, and it had made a different man of him. He was a naturally friendly fellow and a good listener, and what he heard over the years convinced him that workers' overarching concern was not for wages but for job security, and that many were capable of making even greater contributions to the business' success if they understood how the business really worked. As convincingly as any business leader of his generation, Crawford made it his mission to educate them.

It was an unending mission because hostile forces were at work on the left, in government and the unions, offering juicier, more conspiratorial explanations. Crawford believed that the reasonableness of employees was directly proportional to the transparency of their management. He was a "whole truth and nothing but the truth" sort of leader, with a genius for breaking down complicated

Above: Perhaps in response to Roosevelt's New Deal, Crawford launched a Square Deal policy at TP. As national unions pressed to organize workers at the company, posters, such as this one, underscored the idea that workplace grievances could be settled quickly and fairly in-house.

Facing page: Crawford, fist clenched, spoke adamantly against President Roosevelt's New Deal legislation, which he believed threatened the country's free enterprise system. Crawford possessed great skill as a speaker and had a unique ability to motivate people.

MARKET
130,000,000 AMERICANS

CAPITAL

LABOR
130,000,000 AMERICANS

130,000,000 AMERICANS

● Illustrating its position in industry, as propounded by Mr. Crawford, is this sketch showing management to be the integrating force whose task it is to reconcile simultaneous but opposing demands of capital, market and labor. To produce greater wealth for all three, apparently entirely separate but in reality only one, increased production is necessary, says Mr. Crawford, in his defense of the free enterprise system

The Triangle of Plenty

In 1938 Crawford penned an article for *Investment Banking* magazine called the "Triangle of Industry and the Production of Wealth." The piece was an adaptation from a number of speeches he had given on the subject and prompted the creation of the Triangle of Plenty, shown here, to illustrate his belief that the economy worked by satisfying the conflicting needs of consumers, providers of capital, and labor. The article attracted great notice and solidified Crawford's reputation as a champion of free enterprise.

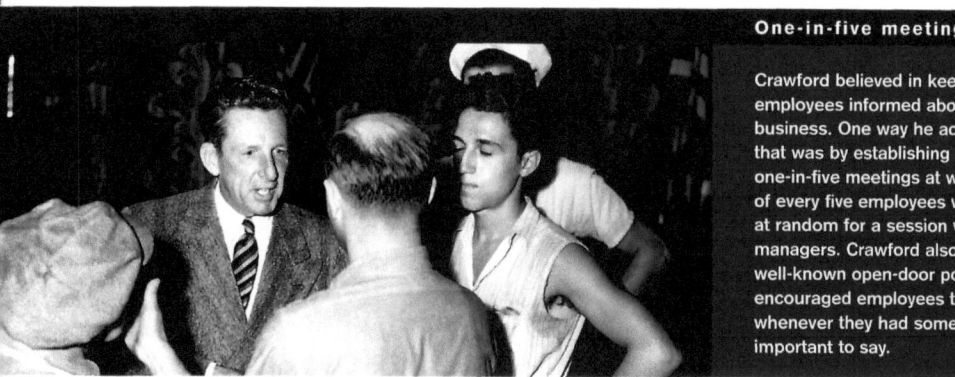

One-in-five meetings

Crawford believed in keeping employees informed about TP's business. One way he accomplished that was by establishing regular one-in-five meetings at which one of every five employees was picked at random for a session with top managers. Crawford also had a well-known open-door policy and encouraged employees to drop by whenever they had something important to say.

economic and business issues into manageable parts that could be explained in plain language that ordinary workers understood and respected. What might have seemed bland generalities about "mutual understanding and cooperation between employers and employees" he backed up with plausible answers to fundamental questions that to this day, in some quarters, unfortunately still beg illumination.

"What is management and what is labor?" he liked to ask audiences of assembled employees. Everybody was a workman, he answered. Everybody came into the plant, effectively punched the clock, did his job, and went back home at night. No one did it because he was crazy about work. But everybody had to eat, pay the rent, put clothes on the family's back. Everybody wanted the company to succeed and have lots of business, and of course everybody wanted more pay. On that count, especially, everybody was in the same boat: "None of us is wholly satisfied. There is no man who works in this entire organization, including management, who gets as much as he thinks he is worth." Plain words with the ring of truth.

Crawford rejected as utterly bogus the divide thrown up between management and labor by the left and pictured instead a company as a group of human beings totally unified in their goals, only with somewhat different perspectives. Everybody did the same job day after day, but management had to think about it more. Management had to think (it was an idea he liked a lot) in "perpetuity." Would, or could, the company last? What was being done today that shortened, or lengthened, the odds that the company would still be around tomorrow?

Management's job was "to perpetuate the institution." At the end of the day, workmen could turn the job off till the next morning when, regular as clockwork, they passed once more through the factory gate. And that very regularity was their most precious treasure. For the successful company supplied not just jobs, but steady jobs. Management too "comes and does its work, but all the time it must worry about whether we will be here next year, whether we are running this year so that we don't go down in defeat next."

If workers learned to appreciate this "yardstick of perpetuity," as he liked to call it, then they would understand better the real burden that management carried. And then, whenever they asked for something (like higher wages), they would understand better that more today might possibly mean less — or nothing — tomorrow.

Crawford liked homespun images and stories, which sound corny today but still make a point. When he talked to workers, he would ask them, for instance, to picture the business as a big coffee grinder. You put in money and oil and steel and taxes and all the other things you could control — except the amount of time that labor then took to make something out of it, which at TP was then about half the total cost. And how to control that? You might, he offered (this was the 1930s), try "Stalin's way, using force and cruelty to get a reluctant day's work." But in America, where the individual was king (or ought to be), the only control that management really had was "in the mind of the worker." It made sense to Crawford that management consider carefully what the worker was thinking about.

The worker was thinking, chiefly, about his job, and he would think about it correctly if he understood what Crawford called the Triangle of Plenty. Crawford was way ahead of his time when it came to thinking about a company's several stakeholders: customers, investors, and employees. All were interdependent, he said, and all could benefit only if production rose and wealth increased.

Henry Ford was something of a hero to him in that regard, and he liked to tell the story of how Ford responded to the big-time success of the Model T. The first thing Ford did was not to raise wages but to lower prices and give the savings to the customers, whose rising numbers quickly created a mass market for automobiles. Then he reinvested growing profits, which lowered prices further and guaranteed thousands of jobs. Then, and only then, did he pay workers more. But when he did, he did so with a bang, doubling what was then considered good pay, to a munificent $5 a day. "If Elijah had seen what Henry Ford did," Crawford put it with awe, "he'd have written three pages about it in the Bible."

Happy factory

At every point in its remarkable history, Thompson Products, and later TRW, has been shaped by and has helped to shape outside events. Ford's "Model T revolution" drove the demand for what TP made, and the price and reliability of what TP made helped drive the revolution. During the 1930s, economic depression and Roosevelt's New Deal conditioned behavior inside TP, and Crawford's fierce reaction in turn gave voice to a fierce reaction in American business at large that crimped the New Deal. Succeeding eras were of course unique, but a similar interaction could be observed during the nation's economic mobilization during World War II, the aerospace defense build-up of the Cold War years, and the defense build-down of the post-Cold War era (see Chapters 3, 4, and 5). At this point (still in the 1930s), it was Crawford's response to an outside challenge, personalized in his arch-adversary Roosevelt, that bequeathed to TP certain characteristics destined long to outlive his and FDR's particular philosophical duel.

With organized labor emboldened by the New Deal, TP came under great pressure during the 1930s to let the unions in. Pro-worker but anti-union Crawford responded with an approach to industrial relations, or "human relations," as he preferred to call it, that stood out in American industry. With American Federation of Labor organizers prowling threateningly at several TP plants early in Crawford's presidency, the company formed what it called the "Old Guard," an organization consisting of company veterans with at least five years' service who drafted a constitution for the Thompson Products Employees' Association (TPEA). A 14-member Joint Council was set up to run the association, with half its members elected by the workers and half appointed by management. The Joint Council was to be the bargaining agent for all employees, and its decisions were binding on all. Arbitration took the place of strikes, which were prohibited. The Joint Council worked from 1934 to 1937, and by all indications it worked very well at the main plant and spread outward across the company.

At the same time, Crawford stepped up communications inside TP and began to professionalize personnel management in ways that

With organized labor emboldened by the New Deal, Thompson Products was under great pressure to accept unions. Management responded by forming a committee consisting of TP managers and members of the Old Guard, an informal group of veteran employees with at least five years of service, to draft a new employee constitution. Among other provisions, the constitution barred strikes, providing instead for arbitration and appeal to the company's board of directors.

Old Guard gathering

Just after Crawford assumed the TP presidency, he formed the Old Guard. Employees regarded the badge worn by members as an emblem of honor.

The association sponsored yearly picnics, banquets, and Christmas parties and provided emergency monetary assistance to employees. This photo was taken at the group's first banquet in 1934. Female members of the Old Guard were recognized at a separate gathering.

Friendly Forum

THE VOICE OF THE EMPLOYEES' ASSOCIATION

Vol. 1 No. 1   CLEVELAND, OHIO   April 2, 1934

WORKERS IN FAVOR OF GROUP PLAN

Closer Relationships Seen as 80% Approve Constitution

BY W. A. HOFFMAN, *Chairman*

Employee Representatives desire to share more fully the prosperity that often becomes a part of a growing concern led over 80 per cent of the Cleveland employees of the Thompson Products, Inc., to cast their ballots in favor of an Employees' Association on January ... There are now 741 members.

This procedure was favored mainly because it creates a closer relationship between the employees and the company. It was seen that affiliation with an outside union could not bring about the results sought as fairly and expeditiously as an inside organization working in harmony with the company.

Outside unions have in the past made demands upon companies that have been detrimental to the employees themselves due to the fact that a considerable volume of the business was actually lost to competitors in other locations, where labor could be secured cheaper.

Situations of this kind can not occur with an inside association fully co-operating with the company. It is this keen interest of the employees in the welfare of the company that will bring abundant returns to them when the business shows profits.

Constitution Drafted

After approving the Employees' Association plan by a large majority, the next step was the selection by secret ballot of five committee members to draft a constitution. This was by no means an easy task and although it appeared to those not connected with the committee that there was undue delay, nevertheless the constitution was completed in less time than is ordinarily required.

The constitution has been printed in booklet form and each member of the association has received a copy.

Employee Representatives Hold Caucus on Plant Affairs

Terms of the Management's contract with the Employees' Association were being discussed ... of an informal factory representatives' meeting was snapped last week. Later, a copy of the ... erly executed was signed by the representatives and filed with the secretary.

Representatives, left to right, are: Al Adams, Louis Gongos, D. D. Tucker (West Side), ... ter (Secretary), W. A. Hoffman (Chairman), T. C. Smith (West Side), Henry Perry, P. N. Miller. Demeter has no vote on council affairs and was appointed by the chairman to handle secretarial matters.

Board Refuses To Order Vote

Union Men Told to Try Bargaining at Hearing

At a hearing before the Regional Labor Board, March 20, a group of company employees interested in an outside union requested an election be held in company plants. The employees were accompanied by Charles Milz, business agent of the Metal Trades Council.

After hearing remarks from both sides, the Board declined to order an election. As the company management had previously expressed its willingness to bargain collectively with members of all groups, the complainants were told to proceed to negotiate. The Board also reserved the right to review this decision in two weeks.

Cox Optimistic

Outlook Good as Plants Work at Near Peak Capacity

West Side plants are operating at near peak capacity and since

Pig and Beer Feature Dept. 6 Feast

Club Planned For Good Times

Rollicking over a ham-roast, approximately ninety employees from Dept. 6 headed by Louis Weber held a get-to-gether last Saturday in the cafeteria.

The idea of becoming better acquainted with fellow workers was promoted, and opinions were heard on the possibility of organizing a department club to plan social and recreational activities.

Kerwin Makes Plans For Handicapped Men

Superintendent John M. Kerwin calls attention to efforts the company is making to find suitable work for physically handicapped employees in order that they may be kept on the payroll. Strict observance of State Industrial Board Rules permits only the hiring of men able to pass a prescribed physical examination.

Company Buys New Equipment

Heald Grinders to Be Used On Seat Insert Line

Two new Heald centerless seat grinders, the most modern of this type of equipment, have been installed on the valve seat insert production line in Department 8, according to J. M. Kerwin, superintendent.

The machines are capable of exceptionally close precision work, and are considerably faster than others formerly used. Scrap is reduced to an absolute minimum, an automatic safety device stopping the machine as soon as a piece jams. The operators' hands are never near the grinding wheel or other moving parts, the work being charged in by a magazine.

Company also has ordered a new 700-ton extrusion press from Ajax Manufacturing Co. This will be in operation within two months in Dept. 20.

Outlook Favorable

Main Plant Sales Should Hold Well, Mr. Clegg Believes

Current rates of activity should

MOTOR PEACE PATTERN FOR PART MAKERS

Already Observing Agreement Principles ...

... oping employer-employee relationships in the automotive parts industry.

Settlement of the threatened automobile strike was based on five major principles to be observed by both industry and labor in future dealings.

"1—The employers agree to bargain collectively with freely chosen representatives of groups, and are not to discriminate in any way against any employee on the ground of his union labor affiliations."

Company in Accord

Present management-labor relationships at Thompson Products are entirely in accord with this item. Management has been negotiating for several weeks with elected delegates of the Employees' Association, numbering over 700 workers, and has expressed its willingness to discuss terms with representatives of any other company groups. There has been no discrimination because of union affiliation.

"2—If there be more than one group each bargaining committee shall have total membership pro rata to the number of men each member represents."

To date is has been physically impossible for management to serve this condition, as the Employees' Association is the only group to submit a membership list. Obviously, management can not pro-rate delegates of other groups when the number ...

The Friendly Forum

Throughout the 1930s great strides were made in improving communications at Thompson Products. In April 1934, for example, the company began twice-monthly publication of an employee newsletter, the Friendly Forum. (The first edition is shown here.) The Forum, which began as "the voice of the employees' association," went on to serve employees and management alike.

soon set the industry standard. He believed in telling employees "everything," was a great believer in mass meetings, and made it a rule that every division manager must talk to his employees at least once every 90 days. The company's twice-monthly newspaper made its debut in 1934. Crawford named it, very deliberately, the *Friendly Forum* and envisioned it as the voice of management and workers alike. In it could be found local news of personnel changes, company picnics, and sporting events, but also editorials about management policies and industry news.

That same year, Crawford selected then 27-year-old Ray Livingstone as director of personnel and charged him to learn fast everything he could and teach everybody else as he went. Livingstone was a systematic sort of fellow who pioneered employee opinion surveys and wage data in figuring out what was really going on in the organization. One of his most important actions was to launch a training program for foremen, who typically wielded great power in manufacturing plants like TP's and who were not known for their gentle ways with workers. "Handling Men," "Placement of Men," and "The Why of a Foreman" were subjects of classes aimed at upgrading management where it mattered most, on the factory floor. Hiring processes became more transparent and humane (the traditional "bullpen" employment window at the plant gate gave way to interviews in a private room). Training programs and handbooks for supervisors and employees all aimed to smooth the rough edges from factory life and keep everyone working steadily and profitably.

None of this, however, could keep labor issues from heating up, particularly after passage of the National Labor Relations or Wagner Act in 1935. This was followed by yet another spate of union militancy that ran head-on into Crawford's iron will to preserve management's independence at all costs. His investment in enlightened "human relations" paid off in the years ahead, as TP employees repeatedly rejected representation by industrial unions.

Crawford never patronized, however, and always said that if employees really wanted unions, then by all means they should have them. He also wanted, for his part, freedom to tell employees unions were a bad idea and that if relations between the boss and the workers were as good as he believed them to be at TP, who needed a third party to tell them what to do? "If the boss is a son of a bitch," he put it plainly, "then employees might need a union to intervene. But I wasn't a son of a bitch."

The proof of the investment in human relations was in the performance. In a time of unprecedented industrial unrest, TP stayed at peace and reaped the rewards. Human relations became the best sales tool the company ever had. "Buy from us and you'll get your stuff on time. We don't have strikes." It was a hard line to argue with, and when Roosevelt's Secretary of Labor Frances Perkins once told Crawford to negotiate with the Congress of Industrial Organizations (CIO), he did not hesitate to tell the good lady to back off.

"Dear Mrs. Perkins," he wrote. "The CIO has just deceived you. And incidentally, if you tend to your business, I'll tend to mine, and we'll get along very well."

Among the company's most enduring publications, the *Friendly Forum* was printed for more than 50 years. A 1951 issue, shown here, recapped TP's first five decades.

1940–1959

3

Stepping up and out

Crawford, left, flashed a smile as he rode beside legendary U.S. Army General Douglas MacArthur. The general (above) visited Tapco in September 1951 and addressed employees as the company launched a $13 million expansion to increase manufacturing capacity for the Korean War.

One of the most famous pictures around TRW from the war and early postwar years depicts not Fred Crawford or Arch Colwell or Ray Livingstone or any other of the inside team that had brought Thompson Products successfully through the Depression, but General of the Army Douglas MacArthur. It is an unposed shot of MacArthur at TP's Thompson Aircraft Products Company (Tapco) plant, delivering a pep talk to workers at the time of the big expansion in capacity to meet demands of the Korean War. Turn back the clock seven or eight years, and it might have been another top brass, no doubt less famous, bestowing on TP an Army-Navy "E" Citation for meeting schedules and keeping up quality in the fight against the Axis powers.

Crawford as a rule did not like government men, but when there is a war on everyone loves a soldier. And MacArthur visited a lot of war plants and met a lot of managers patriotically doing their bit. Crawford and his crew at TP were as patriotic as any; when country called, they answered. Besides, without the war and the government that ran it, there would have been no Tapco plant at all. And that would have left TP a vastly different sort of company from the one it in fact became as a consequence.

Germany and Japan were resourceful, and victory in the highly mobile warfare of the mid-twentieth century depended on technology as much as it did on brave soldiers and bold strategies. Radar, even more than daring young pilots, won the battle of Britain. Atom bombs, which substituted for thousands more pilots, soldiers, and sailors, finally won the battle in the Pacific. Like no conflict before it, World War II was a wizard's war. Like all conflicts before it, it was a war of supply lines. On the companies with the job of actually manufacturing the wizardry and getting out the supplies, it bore down like nothing in past experience with the relentless pressure of change.

TP came of age during this, America's "last good war." It experienced terrific growth. Sales soared by a factor of eight between 1939 and 1944; in perspective, operating profit in 1944 of just over $14 million exceeded the company's entire sales in 1938. But it was not the numbers alone. Bigger scale (4,000 employees before the war became 20,000 at its peak) demanded better management and thinking about the enterprise in fresh ways. Wars come, but wars go. This one, which came on slowly and ended quickly, was a proving ground for performance at that moment and a challenge to look ahead. The experience bought TP maturity ahead of its years and positioned it exceptionally well for postwar opportunities. TP's response transformed what had begun as a largely provincial enterprise into a national and even a global business success story. If ever a company did well by doing good, it was this one.

Duty's call

The "good" in this case was the patriotically determined one of national defense. During the war, America built a vast arsenal to win victory for democracy. After the war was won, America sustained a vast arsenal for deterrence. America wanted never to be caught short, or by surprise, again. So it prepared relentlessly for the next war, which, it prayed, preparation would prevent.

It may have seemed a long way from making engine valves for Model Ts to saving democracy from dictators set on destroying it, but in an age of mechanized warfare and technologically sophisticated weaponry, the connection became clear quickly enough. It became particularly clear with regard to that up-to-then disappointing third leg of TP's business: parts for aircraft engines. For World War II was the world's first truly airborne conflict, its opening to closing images — from the Stukas of Germany's Blitzkrieg in 1940 to the armadas of B-29s that flew over Japan in 1945 — dominated by air power. After watching helplessly the Nazi invasion of France in May 1940, U.S. President Franklin Roosevelt called for a massive increase in America's production of aircraft, first to 50,000 a year, then 60,000, and ultimately 120,000. These were numbers that set lots of heads in the aircraft business spinning, largely with delight but also with worry about where resources would ever be found to accomplish such a feat. The answer was largely from the public coffers, via the Defense Plant Corporation, established early in 1941 under the umbrella of the New Deal's Reconstruction Finance Corporation. Fred Crawford, who hated the New Deal with a passion second to no other man's, suddenly found himself having to do patriotic business with the devil — and liking it.

Roosevelt had tapped General Motors President William S. Knudsen for the job of overseeing conversion of the country's heavy industry to war production, and it was Knudsen late in 1940 who summoned Crawford to Washington to talk about how TP could serve the cause. "We're going to have to make a hell of a lot of valves," he told his visitors (Dave Wright, TP's 35-year-old treasurer, had accompanied Crawford), and his terms for doing so were hard to turn down, even for a dyed-in-the-wool conservative like Crawford. Government funds would build and equip the plants. TP would put up a small amount of capital in the form of equipment transferred from its Clarkwood Road plant, and it would have complete responsibility for design and operations, including recruitment and training of the workforce. For its troubles, TP would get a guaranteed financial return and first place in line to buy the plant at the end of the war.

The result was "Tapco" and the Tapco plant constructed in 1941 on a 120-acre abandoned

Above: The Army-Navy "E" award was given to defense contractors for excellence in meeting production schedules and maintaining quality. Tapco employees, three-time recipients of the prestigious award, were cited for their "meritorious distinguished service and dependability." The September 1943 award presentation drew a crowd of nearly 40,000, reportedly the largest gathering of its kind in Cleveland during the war, to the Tapco parking lot, where Crawford (third from right) accepted the honor.

Facing page: Employees jammed the cafeteria in March 1942 for the dedication of the Tapco plant. Incorporated as a wholly owned subsidiary of TP, the facility was built on an abandoned 120-acre vineyard in Euclid, Ohio, about 10 miles east of downtown Cleveland. Ground was broken in April 1941, and less than eight months later workers, periodically warming their hands over coke fires in oil drums, produced the plant's first sodium-cooled valve.

vineyard in the Cleveland suburb of Euclid. Tapco was set up as a separate subsidiary corporation to protect TP from exposure to sudden fall in demand should peace be declared without warning. With every modern (by 1940 standards) four-engine bomber requiring 144 valves to stay aloft, the new entity had its work cut out. The plant ultimately would cost $30 million and was huge: a sprawling single-story structure enclosing more than a million

overnight and were forced to apply their manufacturing know-how to making different products entirely (machine gun triggers and gyroscopes). TP was fortunate that it could continue making what it had always made, though to new specifications and for somewhat different end products. Even so, the war spurred technological innovation and left TP, at the end of it, on the brink of a future that looked like no mere replay of its past.

Air Force at Tapco

Let's have the truth

Far left: Horace A. Shepard, second from left, stood between Wright and Crawford during a visit by the U.S. Air Force to Tapco. Shepard eventually left the Air Force for a career with TP.

Left: *Let's Have the Truth* bulletins were issued by the company, usually in response to literature from the Congress of Industrial Organizations, which sought to unionize TP. The bulletins regularly used cartoons to portray the company's position on labor issues.

square feet and employing nearly 12,000 workers at its peak, it was a model for its times with bright fluorescent lighting, air-conditioned cafeterias, and parking for 3,500 cars. Ground was broken in April 1941. Construction went fast, but even before the roof was on, Tapco workers turned out their first sodium-cooled valve on December 2, just five days before Pearl Harbor brought the war home to Americans. By the middle of 1943 Tapco's nine production lines stretching over one and a half miles were churning out 400,000 valves every month, which was close to 90 percent of all Allied requirements.

Swizzle sticks and Chevy jets

Conversion to war production meant different things to different companies. Some saw the markets for what they had made in peacetime (washing machines or postage meters, to pick two random but typical examples) vanish

Bright ideas come in funny places. One, for high-altitude fuel booster pumps, occurred to TP "resident engineer" William H. Curtis in the club car of a transcontinental passenger train. Stirring his highball with a swizzle stick, he noticed how the action caused gas bubbles to separate from the liquid and rise to the surface. The same principle, he reasoned, could be applied to aircraft fuel tanks, where the problem was to force the heavier fuel directly into the fuel lines and the bubbles to the top, thus eliminating dangerous vapor locks. It worked, and TP soon found itself, at peak production, turning out 20,000 high-tech pumps a month.

A much greater opportunity, and technical challenge, came toward the end of the war as the United States strove to catch up to British and German advances in jet propulsion. Late in 1944, the Army Air Force placed a large order with General Motors (through

Facing page: At its peak, the Tapco plant was a showcase of 1940s American manufacturing. Originally a half-million-square-foot, one-story factory that housed 5,000 workers, the plant underwent numerous expansions during the war years and grew to more than a million square feet of production space and accommodated more than 12,000 employees. "It was," declared a company publication, "a far cry from the old conception of factories as places of clangor, dust, and gloom." Tapco, in fact, featured miles of fluorescent lighting; indoor plumbing, heating, and ventilation; two air-conditioned cafeterias; employee lockers; and parking for 3,500 vehicles.

General Electric) for British- and American-designed jet engines. GM's Chevrolet Division was responsible for half of it, and it was Chevy general manager Hugh Dean who called Dave Wright, his old friend at TP, over the Christmas holidays asking for help. Dean needed high-quality components fast: compressors, turbine wheels, and shafts. Wright, who had never so much as seen a jet engine, was awed by a single piece of business worth $40 million–$50 million and did not hesitate to accept the challenge. Early in 1945, chief engineer Harry Bubb took charge of a new manufacturing division dedicated to jets, and Tapco headed toward producing a thousand turbine wheels a month.

Recalling prodigies of wartime production, however, does not capture fully the flavor of those times. With the men away, more women than ever before could be found working the assembly lines. And Ray Livingstone launched a pioneer effort to employ African-Americans approximately in proportion to their representation in the local Cleveland population. Repeatedly, the company won important successes against organized labor by keeping up its heavy investment in programs of progressive human relations. And Fred Crawford maintained his high-profile stance as both TP's and Tapco's *pater familias* and as unflinching advocate for the American system of free enterprise capitalism. Crawford's growing public reputation probably strengthened his leadership inside TP. The boss, everyone knew, was known and respected (and by a few, reviled) in the wider world where public policy was shaped, and his reputation gave this still modest-sized Ohio-based manufacturing company a punch beyond its weight.

In November 1942, as American war production was still getting organized and at the nadir of the Allies' fortunes on the battlefield, TP's Fred Crawford reached the top, with election as president of the National Association of Manufacturers (NAM) and selection for the cover of *Business Week* magazine. In the business world, he became a celebrity, carrying the "Thompson Creed" (create the wealth first, share it second, and be guided by the Golden Rule) far and wide across the country. He even served the enemy FDR, voluntarily and patriotically, as a member of the War Advisory Council of Businessmen, the War Manpower Commission, and the Management-Labor Policy Committee. He traveled to Europe twice with business delegations to report from the front firsthand. The folks back home loved it: "He is like the volcano that is creating itself in Mexico," said the *Cleveland Plain Dealer,* "Constantly sending out heat, light, fire, steam, and sometimes brimstone."

Free speech, free men

Sometimes brimstone came hurtling back at him and the men who ran the company day to day in his absence: Dave Wright, Arch Colwell, Lee Clegg, Jim Coolidge, and Ray Livingstone. Three times during the war the unions attempted to organize TP workers, and three times TP management and TP workers beat them off. Crawford had always tried to frame the union problem not as a battle between management and labor, but between the company and intrusive outside forces abetted by the government, and sometimes by

Above left: A call for "unprecedented" cooperation between labor and management during World War II spurred the creation of this advertisement, which appeared on the inside cover of *Time* magazine and Cleveland-area newspapers.

Above right: Crawford's election in November 1942 to president of the National Association of Manufacturers gained him his first cover on a national magazine, *Business Week*. With his usual panache, he helped revive the flagging organization.

Facing page: As the war raged in 1942, TP and Tapco cast aside a general industry reluctance to hire women for manufacturing positions. Two years later, more than one-third of the company's Cleveland-area employees were females who served as machine operators, finishers, and inspectors. Peacetime, however, brought the return of company policy, which included hiring only single females and requiring their dismissal upon marrying.

Diversified workforce

Left: TP was one of Cleveland's first major employers to hire large numbers of African-Americans. The effort came on the heels of a meeting between the company's personnel manager and officials of the city's Urban League. In 1943, at the peak of wartime production, more than 2,000 African-Americans, representing nearly 15 percent of TP's total employment, worked in the company's Cleveland plants.

the government itself. And just months before the end of the war came the test case he long had sought, to pit the claims of an administrative agency (the National Labor Relations Board) against the U.S. Constitution.

The immediate incident involved organizing efforts of the United Auto Workers/Congress of Industrial Organizations (UAW/CIO) in 1944, and Crawford's and Livingstone's highly vocal admonition to TP workers by all means to vote as they pleased, but to be sure they got the facts right first. Crawford posed a simple choice that he believed every worker understood in his gut: sticking with tested leadership dedicated to growth, more employment, and job security versus inviting in outsiders and "all the brawls that seem to follow where outsiders come in." He was persuasive, and the majority of workers took management's side. The trouble (and the opportunity) came when the UAW/CIO protested that Crawford's speeches to mass meetings of "captive" employees on company time interfered with the union's rights to organize under the Wagner Act. When the NLRB sided with the union, scheduled a new election for October 1945, and petitioned the 6th Circuit Court of Appeals to restrain TP's officers from campaigning to TP's workers, Crawford lunged to defend management's constitutional right to free speech. Would a "dictatorial, arrogant agency of government" strong-arm the court into ordering "an American citizen to shut up?"

Happily, it would not. The court dismissed the NLRB petition without comment and gave management a signal victory. The old playful Crawford made the most of it, appearing before each shift in the main plant with a twinkle in his eye: "I wasn't sure I would be here, so I brought this along," he told them, waving a convict's striped suit for all to see. "But it's all right, boys. I don't have to go to jail — the Constitution still stands!"

TP pledge to employees

Facing page: Three times during the war (and several times after) the CIO called for a union vote at Tapco. The efforts failed, largely because Crawford emphasized that no one outside the company could better handle company affairs. TP managers also composed a "pledge" to employees that promised, among many things, the payment of fair wages and the prompt resolution of grievances.

Hot poker defense

The aftermath of World War II in America was odd. Bitter and very recent memories of the 1930s and of the hard times that had followed the end of World War I might have been expected to fuel a "depression psychosis." The loss of wartime production, it was reasonable to fear, would send the country spinning downward to deep recession or worse. But that did not happen. Decisions made at TP as the war drew to a close, and in the early postwar years, tell us why.

To work around Fred Crawford it was hard not to be an optimist. He ran TP from Depression to postwar boom, and he infected everyone around him, and especially his successors-as-leaders, with a steadfast progressive spirit fit for buoyant times ahead. The automotive industry quickly became a shining symbol of America's peacetime manufacturing might, while preparation for wars ahead spawned a vast new sector of American economic life: defense. In the uniform of the peacetime armed forces, the government itself became a heavy consumer of manufacturing output and an important part of TP's future.

Even as America emerged in 1945 as one of the greatest of victors, it took some stomach to take the risks necessary to see that it

"Our Pledge"

We Pledge, as long as the affairs of this company are in our hands, that the following principles will govern our relations with members of the organization:

1. We will pay wages equal to or better than prevailing rates in the area for the occupation. Any employee, or group of employees at any time may request a wage survey to verify the fairness of any rate.

2. With friendliness, we will meet with employees or spokesmen from any group or department to discuss any requested improvements in conditions, hours, policies, or practices.

3. Any grievances will be fairly and promptly settled through steps provided by the Grievance Procedure posted in all departments. Employees may appoint a fellow employee as spokesman if they desire.

4. General conditions such as vacations, overtime, seniority, rest periods, safety, cleanliness, and employee accommodations will be constantly improved, and will always equal, or exceed prevailing community practice.

5. We will devote our best efforts and thinking to the building of a growing business within which will prevail an atmosphere of friendliness and harmony with steady jobs and opportunity for all.

F. C. Crawford

Wartime management

At TP's helm during the war years were, left to right, Ray Livingstone, Lee Clegg, Fred Crawford, Arch Colwell, Dave Wright, and Jim Coolidge.

Cleveland, Ohio
October 18, 1945

Dear Fellow Member of TP:

Will you spend five minutes with me now, a talk seriously and straight from the shoulder, a Thompson Products and you?

My work for the last eleven years has been guarantee square dealing and fair play within Thompson organization. It has been my job to that Thompson men and women receive pay a enjoy conditions of work that are as good or bet than they might receive if they were to take a jo elsewhere in Cleveland.

Ever since 1901, when the business began in a littl building which is now a part of Main Plant, something that is rare and unusual in American industry has been growing within our company: a high mutual regard between men and management—direct man-to-man dealings in an atmosphere of harmony and friendliness—making our company one in which people from all over Cleveland want to work.

This unique relationship, which together we have built, has been founded on natural codes of fair play; on policies and practices which in every instance we believe a neutral observer would hold to be fair.

More than a year ago we reduced to writing the codes, policies and principles that have governed all our actions, posted them in all departments in the form of a simple statement which we call **Our Pledge.**

This was our guarantee to all members of the organization, collectively, of what we promised to each of you as an individual. **This became our contract with you.** Every employee, or group of employees within the company, has to this day the full right to require, in all his relationships with the company, his guarantees under the Pledge.

Has the Company Kept Its Word?

Read the **Pledge** carefully. I think you will agree that it contains all the assurance that any free and independent American might reasonably expect from the company and the job at which he earns his daily living. If this is true, then the issues of this election reduce themselves to simply two:

1. Has the company lived up to its pledge?
2. Is it possible for an outside professional union to promise you truthfully anything more?

would stay on top. For his part, Crawford took the first of those risks in the fall of 1945 when he decided that TP should exercise its option to buy, at the fire-sale price of $5 million, the vast Tapco defense plant. The alternative, as Ray Livingstone recalled Crawford describing it, was "Cape Codizing" the company, which meant going back to making lots of car parts in the main plant, paying themselves well, and spending nice summers on the Cape, where Crawford himself had seaside property. But Crawford's men had come through some tough times together and done things none had thought they would ever be called on to do, and no one was ready to retire quite yet. Taking on the vast Tapco plant, in advance of the orders needed to fill it with working men and machines, they placed a big bet. They won and won handsomely.

Sales and profits proved it. In 1949 revenues of $110 million were seven times their pre-war peak. Two years later, they reached nearly $200 million, which was 50 percent above their wartime high. The key to this performance, and to sustaining it in a change-packed future, lay less with any particular line of products than in the quest for business that fit TP's specialized competence in precision engineering and manufacturing. That was what TP did, whether the result was engine valves or steering gears or turbine blades or (one of the great automotive successes of the postwar years) ball joint suspensions. Surveying the postwar prospects, Crawford and company anticipated both growth and increased diversification. Crawford had long theorized that the replacement parts business, for instance, would be countercyclical to the original equipment market and would help even out the company's overall performance. As the Eisenhower boom of the 1950s got rolling, TP's leaders looked for yet other ways, beyond automotive and aircraft components, to spread the base and guarantee growth.

The man who was key to finding it was lawyer Dave Wright, who had joined the company in 1933 and whom Crawford picked as his successor as president 20 years later. History will probably remember Wright as "the organization man," his persona opposite the flamboyant Crawford's in every way but not a whit less dedicated to the company. Meticulous, analytical, and utterly without Crawford's magical common touch, Wright attended to detail at a level that brings a grin. He reviewed magazine subscriptions in the main lobby and usually cut them back, and he hated so much to waste time that he wore only slip-on shoes so as not to have to bother to tie them. But he knew the business and, like Crawford, cared greatly for the welfare of its people. He was a close student of other big companies like General Motors, DuPont, and General Electric, and he liked to talk about "three secrets of success": decentralization, delegation of authority, and rewards to people in a position to control profits. While Crawford liked to go on about how ordinary people can rise to above-average things, Wright liked people already proven to be bright and brought in some exceptional ones from the outside, like 38-year-old Horace A. Shepard, hired as a vice president in 1951. Shepard was then the youngest general in the Air Force and brought with him established management skills and a network of contacts in the Defense Department and across the defense industry.

In 1952 at the height of the Korean War, about three-quarters of TP's $274 million sales came from turbojet engine components. It was an impressive number and represented mastery of some impressive technology. It was also a perilous number. The postwar defense industry was rich but fickle. As presidential hopeful Dwight Eisenhower promised to wind down the Korean War, aircraft manufacturers and their suppliers (like TP) could expect to experience some wind-down too, or at least

Above: As Wright moved up the corporate ladder, so too did Shepard, who joined the company in 1951. An aeronautical engineer, Pearl Harbor survivor, and once the Air Force's youngest general, Shepard became president in 1962 and was chairman from 1969-1977.

Facing page: Employees in the Tapco tool room in 1944 serviced the machines in the production line by truing grinding surfaces and sharpening cutting tools. The mammoth plant, with round-the-clock operations, accounted for many production achievements during World War II.

Inset: Wright, who joined the company the year Thompson passed away, was Crawford's hand-picked successor, becoming president in 1953 and chairman from 1958-1969. He also was a best friend to Crawford, who once said of him, "Dave has the ability to brush the unessentials away and get at the heart of a problem."

Precision engineering   compressor rotor

TP played a central role in the development of the turbojet engine by fabricating highly complex components. In 1953 the company posted record sales of $326 million, with shipments to the aircraft industry accounting for more than 70 percent of sales. The wind-down of the Korean War, however, forced management to look elsewhere for continued growth.

turbine wheel

compressor inducer

some stretch-out as the services typically decided to take possession of aircraft a year or two later than originally promised. Crawford, ever the plain speaker, put it to a meeting of aircraft industry executives in words that, Shepard recalled, caused quite a stir: "Trying to do business with the government was like having a red hot poker rammed up your rear end, immediately followed by an ice cold douche."

Enter the wizards

Dave Wright's postwar search for growth and a sturdy "fourth leg" to support it turned ultimately on buying into some fast-moving emerging business, where TP had dabbled before but could never hope to play big time by internal development alone. The best opportunity seemed to lie in the electronics industry, which had blossomed during the war but since had shown tantalizing potential in civilian as well as military markets. TP's intelligence and instincts proved correct, although its first foray proved a case of right cause but wrong target. That was Hughes Aircraft, a division of privately held Hughes Tool Company and a California-based plum with a fat backlog of government contracts and, in the judgment of *Fortune* magazine, "a virtual monopoly of the Air Force's advanced electronic requirements."

Hughes fed off the idiosyncrasies of its erratic founder, Howard Hughes, and was a tempestuous company loaded with top-caliber but discontented talent. Among the most discontented were the two vice presidents in charge of operations and research and development, Simon Ramo and Dean Wooldridge. In 1953 TP joined a field of bidders trying to buy Hughes Aircraft. Though Shepard was well acquainted with Hughes' top executives and arranged a highly promising meeting between them and Wright in Beverly Hills, TP could far from afford the asking price (which reportedly ranged up to $50 million) and was wary of dealing with Howard Hughes anyway. The deal died, but something much better soon came of it.

It came in a wee-hours phone call in September to Wright from Hughes general manager and former Air Force General Harold George. George said that he, Ramo, and Wooldridge were jumping Hughes' ship and embarking on their own. They figured they needed close to half a million dollars of start-up money and wanted to know if TP would buy in for 49 percent of their new outfit's stock. Without a pause, Wright said it would. He did not know it then for sure, of course, but with that single conversation he hit the diversification bull's-eye, and he hit it with a howitzer.

Dave Wright liked bright people. In prodigies Simon Ramo and Dean Wooldridge, he and others at TP got to know two of the brightest of their era. They represented a new world of electronics, guided missiles, and spacecraft employed largely in the service of national defense. TP, before the mid-1950s, knew a great deal about precision manufacturing of parts sold to others. After the mid-1950s, it learned a great deal about the engineering of complex technological systems.

Simon Ramo and Dean Wooldridge, both 40 when they launched their TP subsidiary, were brilliant and accomplished scientists and engineers with impeccable credentials. A colleague once marveled, "Working together they are not the equivalent of two men, but something a little closer to 10."

Ramo and Wooldridge made a unique pair. Both had breezed through school and had Caltech Ph.D's in physics under their belts before most men graduate from college. Both came to California to work for Hughes Aircraft right after the war, and both quickly stood out from the crowd. Ramo could have had a career in music (he was an accomplished violinist) but turned to engineering instead. He took mamba lessons to relax and was by far the more flamboyant of the two; Wooldridge played the organ and looked and acted the part of a professor. It was, however, the oneness of their intellects, when it came to matters of science and technology, that was almost uncanny. "We were exactly alike," Ramo put it. "We could finish sentences for each other ... like identical twins."

At Hughes, they had pioneered numerous wonders in military electronics, including the first of its kind "Falcon" air-to-air guided missile system. Probably too bright for any employer, however, they were determined to control their own destinies, which was what led to their proposition to TP late in 1953. They didn't want to be tied up with banks or venture capitalists but sought a partner that could both supply the capital they needed and permit the freedom they needed to use it. TP, which knew its way around government contracting and was experienced in manufacturing and enlightened decentralized management, proved a happy match.

With their TP capital in hand and with Horace Shepard and Arch Colwell from TP on their board, Ramo and Wooldridge set up as the "Ramo-Wooldridge Corporation" (R-W) in a former barber shop on West 92nd Street in Los Angeles, with just two employees besides themselves. They envisioned financing their new company's growth through research and development contracts from the government and other sources, which they hoped would lead to production contracts and expansion into manufacturing. Such a notion of "customer funding" was not one that TP the valve maker had itself ever experienced, but it was well suited to the times and the new subject matter.

Rocket science

How new became apparent within just days of R-W's modest start-up, when Ramo was summoned to Washington by the Secretary of the Air Force to discuss providing technical support for development of the "weapon of the century." This was not, as legend would have it, "the bomb," but rather a new and defense-proof means for delivering nuclear weaponry: the intercontinental ballistic missile (ICBM). The ICBM, which could reach its target a bare 30 minutes from launch and was impervious to countermeasures, revolutionized the strategic understanding of warfare for the rest of the twentieth century. Ramo, Wooldridge, and their new TP colleagues were present at its awesome creation and were partly its creators. They were also present as this apparently unstoppable weapons technology found more peaceful application in space exploration.

As a technical and organizational challenge involving multiple new applications of physics and chemistry principles, the race to build guided missile capability made the wartime Manhattan Project, which had produced the first A-bomb, seem a piece of cake. The decision by the Air Force (which coincided with the creation of R-W) to accelerate the effort introduced a number of new names to Americans' defense vocabulary. First was "Atlas," the program for a colossal five-motor rocket that had suffered early from underfunding and the hostility of the manned-bomber lobby. R-W began the work of evaluating Atlas in October 1953 in what amounted to an unprecedented feasibility study of all the different systems that went into an ICBM: propulsion, structure,

Ramo-Wooldridge logo

Ramo-Wooldridge Corporation

Ramo, left, and Wooldridge began their venture in modest surroundings. They posed in front of their company's first home, a former barbershop in Los Angeles.

The Ramo-Wooldridge Corporation was incorporated in Delaware on September 16, 1953, with TP as a major investor. The agreement gave Ramo and Wooldridge effective control of the company since they elected the majority of the directors.

guidance, reentry. It was this kick that successfully got Ramo and Wooldridge's (and TP's) new company going, and without having to draw on its own (TP's) capital.

The job quickly mushroomed, as R-W found itself confronted with not just providing research and technical support for a revamped ICBM program but also with responsibility for administering it. That meant sophisticated systems engineering and technical direction of the entire vast program. It was a daunting challenge for a still infant firm. The stakes were high, but so was the potential for prestige and professional satisfaction. Looking back, we can detect in R-W's early growth experience an echo of TP's own many years before, when Charlie Thompson's young company had caught the wave of the public's fascination with automobiles and had grown fast and been forced to learn a lot in a hurry. The defense mandate of the 1950s was stronger than any mere commercial fashion, and shoulders bent willingly to the wheel in order to beat the Russians in the Cold War.

The Soviets could be, in select areas, tough competitors, and one of those proved to be missile technology. That technology was highly classified, and because many of the specs for it were determined by R-W, the company agreed to make itself ineligible to manufacture any hardware for the program and, in fact, set up a dedicated new division, apart from everything else, the Guided Missile Research Division, to carry on the design work. As insurance that something would work, alternative approaches were developed to the various systems that made up a missile, and parallel designs were pressed forward as the sense of national urgency increased — "a research program of the highest national priority, second to no others," as President Eisenhower ordered early in 1955. One was the Titan, which would become operational somewhat after Atlas. Another was the Thor, which was an intermediate weapon with a range of 1,500 miles (one-quarter that of an ICBM), meant for forward deployment in Europe.

R-W assumed systems engineering tasks for Thor as for the others. Its new program manager was a 31-year-old Caltech Ph.D. in electrical engineering named Ruben F. Mettler. Mettler had come to R-W just a few months before from a post as senior analyst in the Defense Department and before that from Hughes Aircraft, where Wooldridge had recruited him fresh from graduate school. Like his mentors, Mettler's cool analytical temperament fit him well for the frenetic atmosphere of the missile program, and it was thanks to his management that the first Thor was ready for flight testing just 13 months after start of the program and several months ahead of the rival Jupiter. The launch — before a full-dress throng of managers, engineers, and government officials — took place on January 25, 1957. At the countdown the rocket engine ignited, and the missile lifted tentatively off the pad but then exploded spectacularly.

"Well, we've proven it can fly," offered Ramo, one of the watchers with the most invested and with a good black sense of humor. "Now we just need to work on the range."

More Thors and Atlases failed on test, but Ramo's words were no epitaph. By the end of the year, the missiles flew and flew spectacularly. But so did the enemy's, and on October 4 the Russians sent a chill down America's spine with successful launch of the first earth-orbiting satellite, Sputnik. The event gave birth to a new phrase, "missile gap," with the United States on the wrong side of it, and some high anxiety at high levels about how to close it. The crisis — for it was a crisis ("Sputnik offended and alarmed us," wrote Ramo) — illustrated smartly the interplay of outside events with the evolution of TP and R-W, soon to become TRW. Sputnik confirmed trends already in motion in national defense policy and in new policies relating to

A close partnership existed between R-W and the Air Force's Western Development Command, which was established with "sole responsibility for the prosecution of research, development, test, and production leading to a successful intercontinental ballistic missile." General Bernhard Schriever, left, greeted Ramo, his counterpart as technical head of the ICBM program, in 1954.

Thor missile

Following four unsuccessful launches, a Thor missile finally completed a full-range-and-duration flight on September 20, 1957, making impact 1,300 miles down-range from Cape Canaveral. Jubilation among the R-W/Air Force team was short-lived, however. Two weeks later the USSR announced the successful launch of Sputnik, the first satellite to orbit the earth.

the exploration of space. For ICBM technology could serve to launch satellites and space probes just as well as it could deliver nuclear warheads. In the future, there would be more missiles, satellites, and fancy space communications networks but relatively fewer conventional aircraft, which meant fewer components for the turbojet engines that then were TP's biggest line of business.

External politics thus altered the internal dynamics between TP and R-W, which TP partly owned. Fred Crawford, as head of TP the automotive parts manufacturer, had once made the cover of *Business Week*. But it was, literally, rocket scientists Si Ramo and Dean Wooldridge who, in April 1957, hit the media big time on the cover of *Time*. Tomorrow's technology today had never known such adulation, as R-W symbolized the power of electronics not just to beat back the Russians but also to revolutionize the way Americans themselves lived and worked.

R-W acted quickly after Sputnik, transforming its Guided Missile Research Division into the free-standing Space Technology Laboratories (STL). STL, headed by Ramo and general manager Louis Dunn, was close to many subsequent key space developments. Some of them were fun. Testing a nosecone for an Able rocket, STL engineers exercised the old Crawford touch when, in space designed for a warhead, they placed a live mouse wired for biomedical observation and a two-ounce shot of Old Grand-Dad bourbon bearing the label "Aged in Space." (The first Able crashed, and both mouse and whiskey were lost.) All of it was serious and included feverish work on the early Pioneer lunar probes. STL's growth was almost equaled by the mushrooming commercial business of the General Electronics Group and subsidiary Pacific Semiconductor.

R-W's success left it, however, hungry for capital, which involved it more and more with TP. As early as 1955, TP agreed to provide R-W with a $20 million line of credit in return for an option to acquire 80 percent of R-W's common stock by the mid-1960s. From there on, the fates of the two firms edged closer and closer together. Planning for the second-generation, solid-fuel ICBMs meant to join America's arsenal in the early 1960s aligned them further. As with the earlier Atlas, Thor, and Titan rockets, the Minuteman program saw R-W supply the systems engineering and technical direction. The Minuteman, however, promised to be deployed in hardened silos by the thousands, compared with production of just a handful of the older weapons. The potential scale of the new effort was a strong attraction to units of TP, the seasoned precision-parts manufacturer.

Cutbacks in the Air Force's manned bomber fleet (after Sputnik, half its procurement budget was earmarked for missiles) came just as economic recession two years into Eisenhower's second term dampened sales on the automotive side of TP's business and left it keen, as President Dave Wright put it, "for creating new types of business and opening new markets." R-W's rocket-science-born electronics seemed to offer them. For its part, R-W needed ever more capital to expand the commercial side of its business and hoped for some way to participate in manufacturing the hardware its engineers so expertly designed. Wright, Ramo, and Wooldridge, therefore,

Above: Launched by Russia in 1957, Sputnik "offended and alarmed us," said Ramo. At the time, he was more concerned with the demonstration of Russia's launch capabilities than impressed by the technology. The 184-pound Sputnik resembled a medicine ball in size and carried two radio transmitters that beeped throughout each 96-minute orbit until the satellite tumbled back to earth 21 days later, burning up in the atmosphere.

Facing page: In April 1957 *Time* magazine devoted two covers to the country's missile program. Ramo and Wooldridge were profiled in the second of the two issues, released April 29. The piece brought the pair immediate adulation from Americans fascinated with the era's finest technology.

pushed forward a formal merger, and the new entity, Thompson Ramo Wooldridge Inc., started business on October 31, 1958.

The new name was something of a mouthful and quickly was foreshortened in everyday parlance simply to "TRW." (It was changed officially in 1965.) But the simple name masked a complicated reality. Beyond the strategic congruence of managements' interests, the merger looked like a strange match of Caltech eggheads and Cleveland metalbenders. One partner, TP, was much the larger and had won renown gradually over decades as a master mass producer of precision mechanical parts. The other partner, R-W, was much the smaller and had enjoyed a meteoric rise to celebrity (right onto the cover of *Time*) as a provider of electronics wizardry and engineering know-how for the world of tomorrow. Perhaps sensing the gulf, the two managements agreed at first to leave the two sides of the new firm largely to their own devices in a loose federation. They even retained two headquarters, one in Cleveland and one in Los Angeles.

It was an arrangement, joked Dave Wright, who kept close account of such things, designed chiefly for the benefit of the telephone and airline companies that carried the soon heavy traffic between them.

Wright on merger

Dave Wright was at the helm of TP in 1958 and urged company directors to approve the merger with Ramo-Wooldridge. "There is an ever-increasing emphasis on missiles and electronics in the national defense budget," he said, "and Ramo-Wooldridge is strongly entrenched in both of these fields."

Thompson Ramo Wooldridge Inc.

In the summer of 1955, TP provided a $20 million line of credit to R-W in return for options to acquire more than 80 percent of R-W's common stock. Originally set for the mid-1960s, the merger of TP and R-W was rushed forward under mounting pressure from both companies and completed in 1958. Although officially the Thompson Ramo Wooldridge Corporation until 1965, it wasn't long before the name was shortened to TRW.

1960–1970

4

Two to one, to one too many

There is sometimes more in a name than meets the eye. The name of this new corporation — "Thompson Ramo Wooldridge Inc." — suggested equality between the partners and the smooth fit of organizations just waiting to get together. The country was just then, in 1958, riding out a minor recession. But the postwar boom that saw American corporations vault to world dominion and that made believable illusions of a permanent "age of affluence" still had another decade to run. The best seemed yet to come.

Certainly the spirit of the late 1950s in America, when Thompson Ramo Wooldridge Inc. first set its sails, could not have been more different from the spirit of the early 1930s in America, when Fred Crawford found himself fresh at the helm of Thompson Products with hands full just keeping the ship off the rocks. Yet the victorious run of the war years and the postwar years had not altered one lesson learned in leaner times: If you wanted to stand out from your environment and the hungry competitors who filled it — to lead and not to drift — you had to work very hard at it.

The team that set the pace at Thompson Ramo Wooldridge did so, for the first time, without Crawford, who stepped down as chairman though he remained as a director. This was a watershed, as it would have been in any organization that had experienced the leadership of one such dominant personality for a quarter of a century. But at TRW it was a happy changing of the guard. The younger men now in charge (Dave Wright, who became chairman and chief executive; Dean Wooldridge, who became president but resigned in 1961; Simon Ramo, who became president and then executive vice president; and Horace Shepard, who became vice president and executive assistant to Wright) knew each other well and were all well prepared by Crawford and by their own past experience. One of the things that experience taught was that, however seamless the new name, the "T" and the "RW" parts of the young TRW stood for still strikingly different entities that would probably take some time and imagination to meld into one.

Man on the moon

Facing page: The July 20, 1969, lunar landing was a staggering technological feat in which TRW's lunar excursion module descent engine figured prominently. Performing flawlessly, the engine powered the descent of American astronauts Neil Armstrong and Buzz Aldrin to the moon's surface.

Inset: TRW's new men now in charge (left to right), Simon Ramo, Dave Wright, and Horace Shepard, were well prepared by Crawford and by their own experience. Fully aware that the "T" and the "RW" stood for strikingly different entities, they began the challenging process of forging the two companies into the new TRW.

There were some early stabs at transferring West Coast technology back to the automotive business in Cleveland but, for the most part, without marketable results. Generally, the leadership respected the distinct cultures of its two halves and settled for an evolutionary union that would find its true form in the interaction of their own strategies and events outside the company.

Exit Aerospace

The Cold War and the space race that it begot between the United States and the Soviet Union continued to drive the RW side of the new firm. The escalation of guided missile programs, in particular, pushed TRW to resolve the awkward place of its subsidiary STL and relieve the frustration of not being free to build the hardware its scientists and engineers conjured up and designed. Since the dramatic wake-up call of the Sputnik launch in 1957, the Russians had kept the pressure on and threatened, so it was feared, to deploy an operational long-range offensive missile force as early as 1960. The Air Force responded by forcing forward its own next generation (after Thor and Atlas) of rockets. This was the Minuteman, named for the heroes of Lexington and Concord during the American Revolutionary War. It was to be ready by the summer of 1962 to ward off modern-day threats. STL played a big role that required, as remembered by Rube Mettler, "moving heaven and earth" to meet the new goal. STL did work on the engineering of movable nozzles for the solid-fuel rocket motors, on inertial guidance systems, and on ground support and basing systems. But the Minuteman was also a manufacturer's bonanza, which TRW's Tapco divisions would have dearly loved to harvest and thus offset the concurrent shrinkage of the military's demand for jet engines. Others in the blossoming aerospace industry meanwhile keenly resented what appeared to be STL's (and TRW's) sweetheart relationship with the Air Force.

That relationship, undeniably, was close and worked very well, as evidenced by STL's successful engagement in several experimental (some highly visible and some very secret) government-funded projects that plausibly could have given it a leg up over the competition. Project SCORE, funded by an advanced research arm of the Defense Department and known at first to only a few dozen people (in case of failure), put a mammoth four-ton satellite into orbit late in 1958, which carried a tape-recorded Christmas greeting from President Eisenhower beamed to the world. SCORE, which stood officially for "Signal Communication by Orbiting Relay Equipment," entered the record books as the world's first, admittedly short-lived, communications satellite. Good Cold Warriors all, the engineers who had built it joked that SCORE really meant "Society for the Correction of Russian Excesses." But whatever the meanings, those men clearly knew what they were talking about, as subsequent STL space successes demonstrated. In August 1959 Explorer 6 gave the world an entirely new visual image of a satellite, with its four solar-cell-studded "paddlewheels" that generated enough electrical power to transmit the first television pictures of earth from space. Pioneer 5, launched in March 1960, was another paddlewheel affair but one impressively hurled halfway (22.5 million

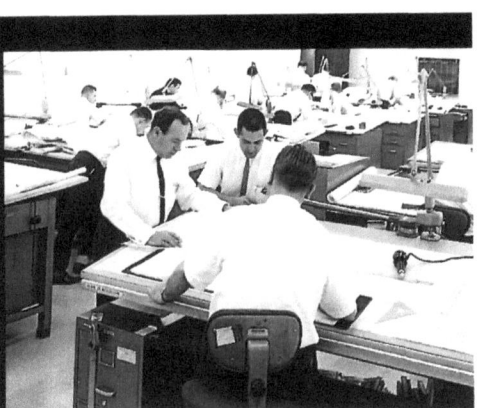

At the drawing board

Space Technology Laboratories played a huge role in the Minuteman program. Bristling with technical challenges, Minuteman stretched the limit of propulsion technology. Engineers worked around the clock to design from scratch its ground support system. Hardened silos had to be developed, and problems associated with silo launching had to be solved.

Minuteman

Left: A 1957 high-level review of U.S. defense policies concluded that the nation was vulnerable to a surprise attack. The Air Force proposed its solution by the end of the year: a new three-stage missile code-named Weapon System Q and soon nicknamed Minuteman. As with earlier ballistic missiles, RW provided systems engineering and technical direction.

Explorer 6

Above: Launched August 7, 1959, the 143-pound Explorer 6 collected data on the Van Allen radiation belts and cosmic rays. Its most dramatic accomplishment was the transmission of the first picture ever made of earth from space — a cloud-covered view of Mexico City.

miles) to the planet Venus with the goal (not quite reached) of achieving orbit around the sun.

Daunting as such feats were to accomplish and daunting as they looked to the public, TRW's difficulty was less technical than it was political. The appearance of conflict of interest, given STL's close involvement with such space programs and its role as systems engineering contractor to the Air Force's ballistic missile program, led in 1959 to Congressional hearings in which both sides vigorously pressed their points. TRW refuted any impropriety but expressed its willingness to get rid of STL, if necessary. The competition claimed the record of STL's business proved it enjoyed an "intimate and privileged position" with its major customer, the Air Force. A specially appointed committee, headed by Caltech professor Clark Millikan, finally recommended that STL's activities be trimmed back to its systems engineering work for the ballistic missile program and that other activities, such as developing boosters and other space apparatus, should be left to "competitive industry." In addition, the Millikan Committee proposed creation of a nonprofit entity (on the model of the RAND Corporation) to take over certain functions required by the military on a stable and continuing basis.

The result, as jointly negotiated in 1960 by TRW, STL (which remained TRW's wholly owned subsidiary), and the Air Force, was the Aerospace Corporation, an independent nonprofit entity incorporated in California. By the terms of the deal, Aerospace became the overnight beneficiary of $20 million of former STL business, along with 1,700 STL employees, many of them highly skilled technologists. It also got, at cost, STL's just-completed R&D facility on El Segundo Boulevard in Los Angeles. In return, TRW got freedom from the ban that had prevented it from competing in hardware for military and space applications.

It was a necessary parting of ways and not a pleasant one for many of the people involved. Longtime STL stalwarts Jack Irving, Al Donovan, and Bud Nielsen, among others, lost an old home to which they rightly believed they had made enormous contributions. Rube Mettler found himself with the toughest job of all, dividing what had been one into two, delicately sorting out who would go where, and trying to ensure that Aerospace had the talent it needed to survive.

But the Air Force had grown to depend on STL's experience and reliable technical performance. As a consequence, STL, even in its trimmed-down format, continued to realize substantial revenues from succeeding generations of guided missile programs.

Space Park

Left: The spin-off of Aerospace was bittersweet. Despite the loss of talented personnel, TRW's wholly owned subsidiary, STL, was left with significant revenues as contractor on ballistic missile programs. As plans for succeeding generations of ICBMs materialized, the Air Force remained heavily dependent on STL, finding it better suited to offer assistance than Aerospace.

Left: STL was faced with the loss of its R&D facilities in El Segundo after the split with Aerospace and broke ground December 7, 1960, on a 100-acre parcel of land, formerly owned by the Santa Fe Railroad. With no major space contracts in hand, Mettler, fourth from left, observed that the project was a "tremendous gamble."

Above: Situated along the northern edge of Redondo Beach, the campus-like complex quickly became known as Space Park and featured an engineering building and three research labs. $7 million was also committed to constructing a straight-line manufacturing facility (not shown) designed specifically for building spacecraft.

Mettler judged that it would be prudent, therefore, to put some physical distance between TRW's missile operations and its expanding civilian space and electronics businesses. For that purpose, he established a separate organization located at Norton Air Force Base in San Bernardino, where 500 TRW personnel moved in December 1962.

STL's renown achieved in the military realm also made it something of a hunting ground for talent, as the civilian National Aeronautics and Space Administration (NASA) geared up for the biggest challenge yet: putting human beings into space. TRW, in fact, almost lost Mettler himself, whom NASA sought to head up the Manned Space Flight Program, a position he turned down, to the great relief of Wright and Ramo. Vice president for research and development George Mueller took it instead. Edward B. Doll, who had headed up program management in the ballistic missile program, also went to NASA and was replaced by Richard D. DeLauer, another Caltech Ph.D., who also became head of STL's Vehicle Development Laboratory and figured prominently in the success of the continuing Explorer and Pioneer programs.

Enter Space Park

Freed to compete, STL set about the task of learning how. Mettler set his highly qualified personnel to making bids fast, and he reorganized STL into five operating divisions and focused planning and marketing on missiles, defense systems, and space programs. But probably his greatest feat up to that point was in persuading TRW to back and to build a manufacturing facility fit for its ambitions to supply the young space flight industry.

Loss of the El Segundo R&D facility to Aerospace increased the pressure to find not just new work space but also space tailored to STL's unique requirements. That turned out to require building for themselves. The land had

once belonged to the Santa Fe Railroad and was located at the northern edge of Redondo Beach, about a mile from the old El Segundo site. Mettler sketched, and architects prepared, plans for a 10-building complex referred to as the Redondo Beach Space Center but quickly shortened simply to Space Park.

And park-like, or at least campus-like, it was. Ground was broken December 7, 1960, on the first four buildings, tagged prosaically after their uses, just as they would still be known 40 year later: "E1" for the first engineering building; "R1," "R2," and "R3" for the first three research laboratories. But the brick and mortar that in Mettler's estimation represented the real gamble was "M1," a big straight-line manufacturing facility dedicated to building spacecraft and itself costing $7 million to construct. Its specs bespoke the extreme demands of building vehicles to go where nothing made by man had ever gone before. These included a 30-foot spherical space simulator capable of handling the largest of spacecraft and roasting/freezing them at temperatures ranging from 275 degrees to minus 325 degrees Fahrenheit in a nearly total vacuum. A special STL-designed carbon-arc lighting system stood in for the sun. A 17,000-square-foot test area put spacecraft through every conceivable trial short of blastoff. As important as how M1 worked was how it was financed, which was without

Above left: Like the country's appetite for space travel and defense products, employment at Space Park grew significantly throughout the decade. Female employees posed with a lengthy printout of the facility's phone directory, underscoring the size of the operation. Space Park continues to house TRW's largest employee concentration.

Above right: When antitrust action forced STL to split, Rube Mettler found himself with a tough job. What had been one was divided into STL and the Aerospace Corporation. It was up to Mettler to delicately sort out who would go where, trying to ensure that Aerospace had the talent necessary to survive.

Facing page: Building vehicles to travel where none had gone before presented unique challenges. A 30-foot spherical space simulator was designed by STL engineers to vacuum test the largest of spacecraft at temperatures ranging from 275 degrees Fahrenheit to minus 325 degrees Fahrenheit.

Horace A. Shepard

In a planned succession, Shepard became chairman in 1969 when Wright, true to his 1961 promise to retire early, stepped down about four months before his 65th birthday. Looking back on his tenure as chairman, "Shep" recalled that he and Mettler "used to spend an awful lot of time together thinking out loud about where TRW stood and what we thought we ought to do."

government support of any kind. This was crucial to Mettler if STL was to make the most of its new freedom and forge ahead to do business with many different military and civilian customers besides its old patron, the Air Force.

Even before M1 was begun, manufacturing wherewithal was key to selling new business. STL beat out seven other finalists in December 1960 to win the NASA contract, worth $23.5 million, to build the first three Orbiting Geophysical Observatory (OGO) satellites. These "streetcars" (as the argot of the trade put it) were designed as big cargo carriers in peaceful service to science, capable of packing into their three-by-six-foot holds 200 pounds of equipment for a variety of experiments. Their solar cells filled large wings that deployed in orbit and that gave the whole strange creation the appearance of a psychedelic dragonfly.

The Cold War tended to blur the boundary between peace and war, and TRW typically did military work intended to preserve the one by preparing for the other. Ramo-Wooldridge had made its name by engineering some of the most fearsome weapons in America's early Cold War arsenal, and TRW's STL carried on in that arms maker's work. At the same time, it contributed to early programs aimed at arms control. In 1961 Mettler's men won the contract for a program known as Vela Hotel. Vela, Spanish for vigil, was a program to design and build prototype satellites to be positioned at altitudes of 60,000 miles on opposite sides of the earth, where they could detect clandestine nuclear explosions, including those in space. The first Vela went into orbit in 1963.

While STL fabricated hardware in M1, its laboratory engineers across the campus worked with ideas whose application still lay a few years in the future. One of those, which at the end of the 1960s would put TRW's name up in lights, involved spaceborne propulsion systems and particularly the need for throttleable, variable-thrust engines that would be required to "soft land" space vehicles on the surface of planetary bodies other than earth. STL lost out to Thiokol Corporation for the job of manufacturing the engines for the small, unmanned Surveyor mooncraft. But much was learned in the process, putting STL in a strong position to bid — and win — the subsequent contract for the lunar module descent engine that would land Apollo astronauts safely on the surface of the moon.

Diversification full ahead

In 1969, the same year that TRW technology helped Americans reach the moon, Horace Shepard succeeded Dave Wright as chairman in a planned succession. "Shep," as he was commonly known, had enjoyed a career of uninterrupted ascent, and when company president and co-founder Dean Wooldridge retired early in 1961 during a downturn in the commercial electronics business, 49-year-old Shepard moved up to the heir-apparent number two spot. His progress surprised no one and was widely approved on both the "T" and the "RW" sides of the company.

Shepard was an impressive character: Pearl Harbor survivor, aeronautical engineer, Air Force general. To the leadership of TRW he brought an enviable combination of substance and style. He was trained at Auburn University in Alabama and had a Southerner's soft affability. He was as friendly, if not as flamboyant, as Fred Crawford. He was also as analytical as Wright and no shirker from making tough decisions. A reporter once asked him to define the top job at TRW. "That's easy," he replied, no doubt a bit too modestly. "I'm everybody's assistant." What he meant was that while it was the job of top-level people to make the big choices, the menu they had to choose from depended entirely on the

Product publicity

Above: It was the 1960s, the age of miniskirts, go-go boots, and hot pants; and TRW's advertising reflected the times. The art of product publicity has evolved dramatically since this '60s-era promotional shot for TRW's satellite technology was taken at Space Park.

Facing page: STL highlighted its yet-to-be-finished Space Park in its first major proposal to design and build a spacecraft — NASA's Orbiting Geophysical Observatory (OGO). On December 21, 1960, NASA chose STL from among eight finalists to construct three OGO satellites. The project helped STL build an early lead in the newly forming spacecraft industry.

people on the front lines whose job was to come up with the ideas. "This company has never been operated by anybody who thought he had all the answers." It was a good model for leadership.

Shepard did, however, have some of the answers himself. He put J. Sidney Webb in charge of troubled Pacific Semiconductor and soon saw a turnaround in the electronic components business. And through the Bunker-Ramo Corporation (a joint venture with Martin Marietta in which TRW was by far the junior member), he gracefully exited the computer business, where he figured TRW could not compete for long against the likes of IBM. Shepard also carried on strategically much in the path set by his predecessors. Diversification, which Fred Crawford had made a first article of corporate faith, worked to combat the ups and downs of market cycles in particular industries and was the key to sustaining the long-term growth and profitability of the firm. Shepard concurred and did his share to correct overdependence on the notoriously volatile business of defense contracting. At the time of the merger, far too much of the new company's fortunes rested on TP's jet engines and RW's guided missiles. A decade later, a healthier picture began to emerge.

In this, the young TRW moved with larger forces that were reshaping American industry as a whole. In the late 1940s, the vast majority of Fortune 500 companies derived the lion's share of their sales from a single dominant line of business. By the late 1960s, far fewer than half would still be so concentrated on their original core. Trends in antitrust partly accounted for the change. As Congress, and eventually the Supreme Court, forbade mergers that reduced competition "in any line of commerce," managers shied from horizontal combinations between competitors and also from vertical tie-ups of suppliers and customers in the same industry. At TRW the new rules reinforced an old instinct to spread the risks around, as the company boldly took up work that it had not done before. The aim was to get into new product lines in commercial, not defense areas, and so diminish dependence on government business. In April 1964, the company acquired a leading manufacturer of precision bearings for transportation and general industrial use, the Marlin-Rockwell Corporation. At the same time, it bought an Indiana manufacturer of manual and power steering gears, the Ross Gear and Tool Company. Neither was huge, but they were not puny either: Marlin-Rockwell employed 3,200 people in three plants in New York and Connecticut; Ross Gear employed 1,600, owned subsidiaries in Brazil and Switzerland, and had substantial investments in Canada, Europe, and Australia.

When Shepard was still president and Wright chairman, Shepard liked to joke that his job was to make the money, Wright's to spend it. The acquisitions indeed cost money, but it was money that TRW could not afford not to spend. Ramo (as vice chairman until 1978) for his part took on an increasingly visionary role and gave great attention to technology developments and systems that could help integrate the company's increasingly diverse operations. The decentralized, informal leadership style established long before and in a much simpler setting by Crawford, continued under Shepard, who organized the diversifying company naturally according to a group structure based on the similarity of markets served. On the former TP side, Edward P. Riley headed up the Automotive Group, which comprised engine and chassis parts (including valves, where it all began), the replacement business, the Canadian subsidiary Thompson Products, Ltd. (which, alone, retained the old Thompson name), and a growing list of overseas operations and joint ventures. Stanley C. Pace ran the Tapco Group with its jet engines and pneumatics.

In 1964 the company, intent on growth and diversification, completed a merger with Ross Gear and Tool Company Inc., of Lafayette, Indiana, a leading producer of steering gears for trucks. Ross Gear brought TRW annual revenues of $32 million, 1,600 employees, and two plants in the United States. With subsidiaries in Brazil and Switzerland as well as affiliates in England, Australia, France, and Canada, Ross Gear further bolstered TRW's global position.

Stealing energy from the sun is the function of this solar power conversion system, being developed for NASA by the Tapco Division of Thompson Ramo Wooldridge. Called Sunflower, the system folds like an umbrella inside the nose cone of the satellite at launch. Once the vehicle is in space, Sunflower opens up, catches and concentrates the sun's rays on a boiler that vaporizes liquid mercury, driving a turbogenerator that will produce 3,000 watts of electric power continuously for at least a year. Sunflower may help power space missions to the moon, Mars, and Venus.

TRW featured in *Fortune* magazine

The February 1963 edition of *Fortune* magazine characterized the newly formed TRW as "Two Wings In Space." Author Robert Sheehan observed, "Thompson Ramo Wooldridge is a product of a marriage, a few years back, of two strikingly dissimilar companies: the glamorous Ramo-Wooldridge 'think factory' created by two young California space scientists in 1953, and staid, 62-year-old Thompson Products of Cleveland, a mass manufacturer of precision parts and components for the automotive and aircraft industries."

On the RW side, Rube Mettler ran STL as a high-tech kingdom unto itself, and Sid Webb tended the Electronics Group, which was made up of everything else that remained on the West Coast.

Group executives enjoyed a great deal of autonomy. "That way, we thought they'd perform better," Shepard put it straight. And performance was important as the diversifying TRW came to differ more and more from its predecessor companies. Below the top, a new generation of managers was coming into place. Retirements in the middle 1960s saw the last of the old guard depart the scene: Arch Colwell in R&D; Ray Livingstone, who had more or less invented human relations at the old TP; Ernie Brelsford in finance. Younger men, typically with fancier educations and brought up in the pressure-cooker atmosphere of R-W's growth years, replaced them. They inherited a company with roots both in America's old industrial heartland and on its far coastal fringe. And before their time would be up, they would come to experience TRW, genuinely, as one company. Given diverse roots and diversified activities, it was not always easy to communicate that unity to the outside. But a major step forward was achieved with official shortening of the name to "TRW" in 1965 and with the launching of a campaign to create a company brand that, it was hoped, would be around long after anyone but historians even remembered who Thompson and Ramo and Wooldridge were.

Not just any conglomerate?

Image ads promoting the new brand in the late '60s touted TRW as a billion-dollar high-tech growth company, an "active but usually unseen force" in the nation's economy, and a "new kind of corporation" whose scientific and manufacturing know-how fueled the growth of several other major industries. TRW diversified at a dizzying pace and became a company of companies producing, to say the least, a wide array of products and services, from valve train parts and forgings and castings to biomedical testing equipment, spacecraft, and classified information systems. It diversified by buying diversified companies. Acquisition of United-Carr in 1967 brought in domestic and overseas operations in fasteners, switches, and electrical controls; United-Greenfield a year later added industrial and hand tools

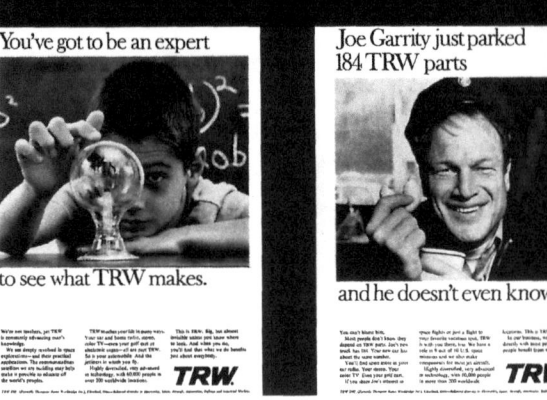

and industrial machinery and equipment to the mix.

Top executives went to some pains to distinguish between their diversification strategy and the strategies that elsewhere then were producing unwieldy and ultimately unsuccessful conglomerates. Every acquisition, they argued, related to existing capabilities. They talked about a strategy of organic growth and defined key terms such as "systems engineering" liberally enough to make a lot of things fit — and to make TRW look like a technology leader across a range of businesses.

One of the hallmarks of TRW during those years was application of systems approaches learned at R-W in the early missile programs to the general management of a fast-growing diversified firm. "Space-age management," as the business journals and popular press viewed it, soon elevated TRW to the pinnacle of forward-looking corporations. There was even

---

Building an image

TRW? What's that? Image ads of the late '60s and early '70s touted TRW as a billion-dollar high-tech growth company, an "active, but usually unseen force" in the nation's economy, and a "new kind of corporation" whose scientific and manufacturing know-how fueled the growth of several other major industries. During this period, TRW diversified at a dizzying pace and became a company of companies producing an array of products and services.

TRW's Poppy Northcutt keeps bringing astronauts home.

TRW...that's a little sports car, isn't it?

No. TRW isn't a sports car.
Or any car. But it is part of a great many cars.

And a great many other things you can enjoy.

A color TV show, a baseball game on radio, a jazz band on stereo.

A plane trip to Mexico. The thrill of a launch into space. Even a ride in a little sports car.

Highly diverse, very advanced in technology, with operations in more than 200 worldwide locations.

This is TRW.

As a leader in components and systems for electronics, space, aircraft, automotive, defense, and industrial markets, TRW doesn't even deal directly with most people. But we're directly involved with almost everything that does.

TRW
Formerly Thompson Ramo Wooldridge Inc.

the imprimatur of a widely circulated set of Harvard Business School case studies on just how TRW managers were molding the industrial organization of the future.

This was flattering, but also deceiving. How TRW managed did not automatically answer the question of what TRW did — or should do next. This was especially touchy with the West Coast "rocket science" side of the company, which had developed such formidable skills in systems engineering and program management in the course of defense contracting. Could such capabilities be applied, and sold, generally in the nondefense economy? STL had already moved into spacecraft, a business similar to missiles, and Mettler hoped that with intensified marketing, other opportunities would blossom.

Ramo and Mettler also urged the TRW Systems Group to seek out private-sector commercial business, and in 1968 they formed an Industrial Operations Group to focus on the "civil market area." The control of industrial processes and instrumentation was natural for TRW engineers, but it was the rising field of information technology, a long-standing favorite of Ramo's, that pointed to perhaps the largest "civil" venture of all. Ramo had a glowing vision of the coming of a cashless society, where software and computers would change the means of economic exchange. His prediction was partly right, and convincing enough to Mettler, who himself had been looking to align TRW with information-intensive businesses where new electronic data processing technologies still waited full application.

In 1968, while young radicals proclaimed flower power to skeptical Chicago policemen, turned campuses into antiwar battlegrounds, and protested generally against the unjust world that industrial capitalism seemed to have handed down to them, TRW took a step of its own toward the coming information revolution. It acquired a small San Francisco–based company, Credit Data Corporation, founded in 1930 and the leader in the yet to be consolidated field of credit reporting. It was an industry that needed some help. Small independent credit bureaus still kept information on index cards, and routine credit checks could take weeks or even months to complete. Mettler saw the acquisition, however, strategically and hoped to learn whether TRW might be able someday to create large proprietary databases and command a leading position in a big future industry. It was, he knew, "a high-risk type of business" but where the dangers were outweighed, he hoped, by "high growth and profit potential."

Historic strength

The answer to the question of "What should we do now, and do tomorrow?" was twofold at least, and what outsiders tended to notice most about TRW during the 1960s disguised the successes of the company's oldest and, in ways, most reliable business. Ed Riley was not a press-conscious personality, but under his nose-to-the-operating-grindstone brand of leadership, the TRW Automotive Group climbed to new technological heights and tackled new market terrain. At home, Riley followed predecessor TP's well-trod path as supplier to America's ever-expanding automotive industry. The irresistible appeal of personal mobility first captured by the mass-produced automobile early in the twentieth century was a magic that never wore off. The magic of capturing its business and commercial potential depended on the ability of companies to penetrate markets further, improve manufacturing efficiency, and keep the stream of product innovation flowing briskly. TRW rose to the challenge with new materials and designs and the introduction of closely related parts. Better technology translated into longer wear and greater vehicle reliability. The "greased-for-life" permanently

In 1966 a *Business Week* feature story gave TRW's management team a well-earned pat on the back: "After years of corporate schizophrenia at TRW, the Cleveland automotive parts supplier and its Los Angeles electronics partner have learned to live together profitably."

TRW Ehrenreich

Through investments and subsidiaries, TRW had manufacturing facilities in nearly all of the world's major automotive-producing countries by the mid-1960s. In response to this rapid growth and to take advantage of a world marketplace, TRW established an Automotive International Division in 1965.

One of the division's priorities was to strengthen TRW's position in Germany. The purchase of Ehrenreich & Cie., a major German producer of steering systems and a key supplier to Volkswagen, was a first step.

Right: Ehrenreich, with headquarters in Düsseldorf, Germany, was acquired in 1968. Cost? About $47 million.

lubricated steering linkages, introduced in 1959 by the same engineering team responsible for ball joint suspension, used new materials like DuPont's Teflon and new types of seals to turn out a product that required no routine service at all. While this made for some unhappy service station and garage owners, who lived by repairs, it also changed standards of consumer expectations across the entire industry that would never be changed back again. The big carmakers extended their warranty policies in the mid-1960s beyond anything before thought possible or wise, and TRW components played a critical role in helping them keep their promises.

Riley's operation also broke important new ground far from home. Acquisitions and joint ventures, plus establishment in 1960 of an international division and a wholly owned subsidiary headquartered in Geneva, signaled the company's decisive response to the postwar prosperity that had put millions of Europeans behind the wheel for the first time. By the middle of the decade, annual production of automobiles outside the United States exceeded what was being churned out by Detroit's Big Three, and manufacturers in several European countries began to grow even faster than their American counterparts.

The Big Three themselves were looking to expand in Europe, Latin America, and Asia and understandably wanted their suppliers to follow suit. But that was not all. Bob Burgin, whom Shepard and Riley put at the head of the TRW Automotive International Division in 1965, foresaw development of a worldwide automotive marketplace and grasped the importance of supplying not just the American Big Three as they ventured overseas, but of also reaching out to rising European and Asian producers. If the market was looked at in that way, the opportunities skyrocketed and bade TRW, which had decades of experience already in supplying the world's largest single automotive market (the United States), to replicate that feat and become the global leader in its strongest product lines of engine valves and steering and suspension systems.

The sporty 1973 Mustang II was the first U.S.-made vehicle to offer power rack and pinion steering as an option.

In order to meet European and Asian demand, Burgin made acquisitions or worked out combinations in Germany (notably Ehrenreich & Cie., a producer of steering systems and key supplier to Volkswagen), Australia, and even Japan, where protectionist regulations restricting foreign investments typically hindered the American challenge. Even so, TRW clawed out an important toehold, through a partnership with Tokai Cold Forming Company, which produced ball joints and chassis parts for the original equipment and replacement markets. By the end of the decade, the results pointed to a healthy reordering of strengths within the company, as TRW established its position as a vastly bigger and more competitive player in the automotive supply industry than it had been at the time of TP's merger with R-W. Its plants and technologies supplied most of the leading manufacturers around the globe, and it operated in every major automobile-producing nation of the Free World.

Management challenge

Diversification, plus strength at the core, did not mean, however, that TRW had found the keys to surefire growth. Even as some members of the family soared, others lagged. Indeed, the outside forces that benefited one part of the firm sometimes harmed another. That was certainly true of the shift in America's strategic defense policy, away from manned bombers to ICBMs. STL profited. But the Tapco group suffered, as sales to producers of jet engines and the makers of military aircraft dropped off. Increased procurement for the war in Vietnam helped somewhat, but compared with the Korean build-up 15 years before, production rates were not high. Technology too could be a kind of villain. Bigger and more powerful jet engines meant fewer engines per aircraft — and fewer total precision components. The first commercial jets, the 707s and DC8s of the late 1950s and 1960s, had four engines apiece. Succeeding generations generated far greater power with just two or three. On the electronic components side of the business, it was equally necessary to adapt artfully to changing markets, and Sid Webb worked hard to sustain R&D investments and grow through acquisitions. The consumer electronics industry was then booming, and TRW components found their way into millions of radios, stereos, and especially color television sets, all of them still "made in the USA." But it was a fiercely competitive market, and TRW did not hesitate to secure a low-cost manufacturing advantage by establishing, early, offshore component plants in Mexico in 1962 and in Taiwan in 1966. By the end of 1968 the group's organization reflected its markets in the military, industrial, and commercial sectors, which together brought to TRW $150 million worth of business and were growing.

Each year Wright, Shepard, and their group and division managers held intensive planning meetings to develop goals for the future. They believed in stretching themselves. In 1967 they said they wanted sales of $2.2 billion by 1970 and $4.5 billion five years after that. Since Crawford took over during the Depression, the company had achieved an annual growth rate of about 18 percent, a number they needed to push even higher. But the 1970s, which slapped America in the face with recession, wage and price controls, the end of the gold standard, energy crises, and shifting patterns of world trade and industrial competition, packed some surprises for TRW, as for many other American companies grown fat in the 20-year postwar boom. The best ones woke up fast. TRW, which was one of the best, saw its strategy of diversification — in 1970 the company had 55 separate divisions — put to the test.

It was Rube Mettler, who succeeded Shepard as president and chief operating officer in 1969, who chiefly got to wrestle with those troubled times. While TRW continued to prosper, with record sales in 1974 of $2.5 billion and net income of more than $100 million, life was not easy. In 1971 the company failed for the first time to set a new earnings record. TRW spacecraft, such as Pioneers 10 and 11 and the Viking probe to Mars, may have continued to capture the public's attention, but the aerospace recession devastated Space Park and signaled that some change of course might well be in the offing.

Mettler had come into the Ramo-Wooldridge side of the company in 1955, where, in the course of supervising various guided missile and satellite programs, he had mastered the tough dual role of scientist and businessman. He had learned that success demanded the best brains, but also the best antennas. As the leader of all of TRW (he became chairman in 1977), Mettler focused fresh attention on the company's external environment and looked for better ways to measure the performance of its diverse members. He shifted to return on assets employed as the new corporate

Above: Ronald Reagan, left, as governor of California in 1966, visited Space Park and met with, among others, Rube Mettler. As U.S. President in the '80s, Reagan supported a defense buildup that benefited TRW.

Facing page: In the '60s the company specialized in developing electronics-oriented hardware. Female employees in the "clean room" at Space Park micro welded and assembled parts for receivers, amplifiers, and power integration circuits for use in OGO and other spacecraft. This photo originally appeared in a 1963 issue of *Fortune* with a caption that described the employees as "nimble-fingered girls, in laboratory dust-caps and gowns, who operate their featherweight machines in an environment more suggestive of a hospital than a shop."

Lunar lander

At the time of the Apollo missions, TRW was running an ad campaign with the slogan "The last 10 miles are on us." The slogan referred to the final 10 miles to the moon's surface, which the astronauts traversed in the LEM, powered by TRW's descent engine.

common denominator of value and relentlessly challenged managers to craft good ideas into long-term profits.

As the spacecraft industry matured, TRW learned how to capture some of the best of what NASA still had to offer. After the triumphs of the first moon landing in 1969 and the epic rescue of Apollo 13 astronauts in 1970, thanks to the stunningly successful and unorthodox use of TRW's lunar excursion module descent engine, the company more than kept up the technological pace and built foundations for renewed growth. In addition to the Pioneer and Viking interplanetary probes, TRW technology drove NASA's High Energy Astronomy Observatory program and the Navy's Fleet Satellite Communications system. And in concert with McDonnell-Douglas, TRW contributed landmark software to the new area of antiballistic missile defense, with the Site Defense program to protect United States launch sites from missile attack.

The correctness of the strategy of diversification seemed confirmed as rising sales on the automotive side of the business compensated for the discouraging downturn in aerospace. New product lines and international expansion figured importantly in this performance.

One small acquisition in 1972 proved particularly astute in both regards. That was Repa Feinstanzwerk, a German manufacturer of seat belts for Volkswagen and other big German automakers. The deal involved an investment by TRW of $8 million in return for a 70 percent interest, with the option to acquire the rest. It introduced the rising business of occupant restraint systems, which in time would become one of TRW's greatest success stories. Rack and pinion steering also came from Europe, through TRW subsidiary Cam Gears Ltd., and began to make an impact in North America as U.S. automakers introduced smaller vehicles in the 1970s.

And when a team of TRW engineers in Michigan, the UK, and Germany came forward with a power-assisted version of the rack and pinion system that suited American driving tastes, it soon set the industry standard.

The computer and data processing businesses that had once looked so promising fell short of fulfillment, however, as the U.S. consumer electronics industry, a major segment of TRW's customers, slipped into terminal decline. Something else in precipitous decline at the middle of the 1970s was the company's stock price, which from a high of more than $43 in 1971 fell to just over $10 by the end of 1974. TRW's business, protected by the strategy of diversification, seemed to be weathering whatever external shocks the world could throw its way. But this apparent operating success was not reflected in the value of TRW to its owners. This irony challenged sharply TRW's managers and foreshadowed a different response in the years ahead.

Above: STL engineers inspected the Fleet Satellite Communications system. Known as FLTSATCOM, the program entailed building a communications network for the U.S. Navy (hence the word fleet) to link naval aircraft, ships, submarines, ground stations, and the Pentagon.

Facing page: Development of the lunar excursion module descent engine (LEMDE) for the Apollo missions to the moon became TRW's most significant contribution to NASA's manned space program. NASA's official history called the LEMDE "...the biggest challenge and the most outstanding technical development" of the entire program.

1970–1998

5

No one ever imagined that TRW's lunar excursion module descent engine would be needed to bring astronauts back to earth. But three weeks after it returned Apollo 13 from its near disastrous mission, crew members Jim Lovell, Fred Haise, and Jack Swigert stood before TRW's Space Park employees with words of thanks. Lovell won a loud ovation by suggesting TRW change its advertising slogan to "The last 300,000 miles are on us."

Refit and reward

NATIONAL AERONAUTICS AND SPACE ADMINISTRATION
MANNED SPACECRAFT CENTER
HOUSTON, TEXAS 77058

October 29, 1970

CB

TRW/Apollo Team
1 Space Park
Redondo Beach, California 90278

On the occasion of our visit with you, following the Apollo 13 mishap, our crew felt there should be something to commemorate our deep appreciation for your efforts in our behalf.

It was only through such dedication as yours that we were able to return safely after the mishap.

We ask you to accept this token of our lasting gratitude, and want you to know we will always recognize the invaluable part the TRW Team contributes to our nation's space program.

Thank you.

[signatures: Jim Lovell, Fred W. Haise, Jack Swigert]

The Apollo 13 astronauts expressed their appreciation to TRW employees with a letter of thanks that read, in part, "It was only through dedication such as yours that we were able to return safely …."

One of ten brothers and sisters, Rube Mettler had grown up in a crowded house. He learned there the virtue of suppressing one's own ego for the good of the whole, and that decisions about rationing resources among needful claimants (the Mettlers were far from wealthy) were seldom easy to make. As TRW's top manager in the 1970s and 1980s, he had ample opportunity to apply those lessons. For by that time, some thoughtful rationing was needed if the TRW family was to continue to grow healthily. The depressed stock price and end of America's quarter-century-long postwar boom demanded some choices.

TRW could, Mettler judged, do a few things well, like the domestic and international automotive business, contract work in space and defense, and perhaps data communications. "But not all the children could go to college."

The big question that dominated Mettler's thinking at this juncture was the tough one of whether or not TRW really was doing what it said. On the one hand, there was what the company claimed: that its widely diversified operations really were intelligently related to core technological capabilities. On the other hand, there was the danger that diversification had gone too far. Had a time-honored strategy passed the point where it merely protected the company from the ups and downs of business cycles and produced a too decentralized organization that defied effective management and, while chasing the chimera of growth, created little value?

Target practice

The answers did not come all at once. In 1975 the top leadership set forth ambitious financial targets that meant getting choosy and indeed "limiting further diversification to exceptional circumstances." And in 1978 and 1979 they followed up with a comprehensively revised set of priorities for the corporation, which were published as *TRW and the 80s*. This document was far more specific about how TRW should meet its goals and spoke directly about needed improvements in quality, productivity, and management development. The link between innovation and market leadership was a prominent theme, and it dictated a fresh look at diversification. How could diversification reach its "optimum" level?

Shifting strategy reflected response both to outside challenges and the influence of fresh management insight. In America's bicentennial year, which also marked the 75th anniversary of the start-up of Cleveland Cap Screw, TRW's board of directors accomplished yet another smooth leadership transition. Upon Shepard's retirement the following year, Mettler would succeed him as chairman and chief executive, while Stan Pace would take Mettler's place as president. Pace brought to the table skepticism about the old tradition of decentralized management, which reinforced Mettler's new caution about excessive diversification.

Seat belts

A pioneer in seat belt technology, TRW introduced an innovative pretensioner device that retracted to take up the slack in seat belt webbing in certain crashes.

This proved to be a theme for the future, in no small part thanks to the rise of another, much younger executive, Joseph T. Gorman. Gorman was a Yale-trained lawyer who had first encountered TRW (actually the old TP) in a course on labor law while studying the Fred Crawford free-speech case. He first worked for TRW in the 1960s era of expansive acquisitions, when Shepard took notice and made him corporate secretary in 1970. Gorman was then 32. That seemed a bit on the young side to some board members, but not to Shepard, who had been made a general in the Air Force at the same age. "I never thought I was too young, and I don't think you're too young," he told Gorman. "So come on in and do the job." The job took him quickly upward; he was a corporate vice president within two years and soon general counsel. One of his early actions in the corporate law department in the early 1970s was to centralize operations and tighten up responsibilities to achieve consistent high-quality legal work across the widely diversified organization. It was a portent.

By the late 1970s, however, Gorman had come to play a role that reached well beyond his job as a lawyer. Much as Mettler, the Caltech rocket scientist, had once served as a sort of internal consultant on strategy to Wright and Shepard, so Gorman, the Ivy League lawyer, now served Mettler. It put him close to the heart of the organization, and he began to take a larger and larger hand in scouting the path it should follow. *TRW and the 80s*, with its comprehensive review of management philosophy and detailed exposition of how TRW should actually reach its goals, bore his mark.

Setting the stage

In the early 1980s outside events clashed with comfortable internal arrangements in ways that prompted at last the beginnings of a

Mettler and Gorman advance new policies

Across the company, Mettler, above, and Gorman, right, advanced a number of new policy initiatives aimed at raising the bar for everyone — from top executive to line worker. Markets were becoming less forgiving, and not all the sound strategy in the world assured success unless reinforced by the right corporate culture.

A company called TRW
Telling our story on TV.

SCIENTIST A: How long do you need to look at a Martian organism before he'll tell you he's there?

NARRATOR: You're one of the TRW scientists who's worked for years

to build an incredibly complex lab, designed to look for life on Mars.

Now the time has come, and you have to ask yourself questions...once again.

SCIENTIST B: Is the temperature we picked too warm for Martian organisms?

SCIENTIST A: Do the organisms only like hostile cold places or are they happy to come out for a warm day on the beach?

We don't understand a biological system that doesn't operate without water.

SCIENTIST C: Running water isn't there now but it sure looks like it was there.

SCIENTIST A: If Mars life only lives under rocks and comes out at night...

we will be sampling from open spaces during the day -- and we'll miss!

NARRATOR: Soon the answers will start crackling back through space, as the search for life beyond Earth begins.

far-reaching corporate transformation. It was not surprising to find Joe Gorman take the point in this process. For even as diversification appeared to help TRW successfully weather the worst recession of the postwar era (as commercial business slipped, defense contracts boomed under the defense buildup of the early Reagan years), it was also becoming apparent that diversification and decentralized ways of doing business masked fundamental weaknesses. In 1984 Mettler tapped Gorman as TRW's next president and, by tradition of succession, his heir apparent to the top job of chairman and chief executive. For the time they remained together, this team navigated TRW through rougher waters than any it had encountered since the Great Depression.

They pushed forward changes aimed to make TRW's organization better reflect the markets it served, and better able to bring its formidable technological arsenal to bear on fresh but often fast-moving targets. One of the biggest and most noticed moves was the merger in 1983 of TRW Electronics with the operations at Space Park to form an Electronics and Defense sector. Mettler argued that the synergies between the aerospace and commercial electronics businesses were compelling and should have been captured sooner. Within new structures and all across the company, Mettler, Pace, and Gorman at the same time advanced a number of new policy initiatives aimed at raising the bar for everyone — top executive to line worker — ever higher. Markets, the leadership correctly sensed, were becoming ever less forgiving, and not all the sound strategy in the world assured success unless reinforced by the right corporate culture.

New experts appeared at headquarters, often from the outside. To direct initiatives in quality, productivity, technical services, and manufacturing, science and technology vice president John S. Foster brought in renowned quality expert John Groocock from ITT, productivity authority Henry Conn, and former Defense Department Under Secretary for Research and Engineering and MIT professor Arden Bement. They wrote down goals for each unit, established formal training programs to raise awareness and improve understanding, and introduced systems to measure progress. Company-wide councils of some 200 division employees assisted top corporate and operating executives in guiding the programs and seeing that change reached far down into the organization. The procedure, they hoped, would become habit-forming.

The phrase "quality cost," for example, soon became a corporate commonplace. What did it cost, anyway, to turn out defective products? TRW, like TP before it, had always boasted to itself and its customers that if it bore the "TRW" brand it was by definition top of the line. But as with many other American companies that had prospered so happily through the 1950s and 1960s when global competition was nil, the quality awakening of the 1980s came not a moment too soon. TRW set a tough corporate goal of trimming its quality costs by 10 percent each year and truly living up to its image. It tackled productivity issues with the same vigor, employing sophisticated new measures for each of the factors of production — capital, labor, material, and energy. Teams tracked results quarterly and benchmarked performance against peer companies and key competitors. The results were soon evident, particularly in the automotive and industrial businesses, where measurable gains in competitive performance gratified executives and invested rank and file with freshened pride in jobs well done today — and to be done even better tomorrow.

How well employees performed and how they felt about it were the specific subjects of an enhanced effort in the area of corporate

Above: In July 1985 TRW headquarters was moved from the Tapco complex to a 180-acre forested estate, formerly owned by U.S. Representative Chester Bolton and his wife, Frances, in Lyndhurst, Ohio. (Coincidentally, the Boltons once were TP shareholders.) The facility accommodates 700 employees and offers 460,000 square feet of office space.

Facing page: This advertisement was one in a series of highly successful television commercials developed to tell the TRW story. The campaign's central theme, "A company called TRW," became one of corporate America's most memorable slogans.

Pioneer 10

Launched in March 1972, the 9.5-foot, 570-pound Pioneer 10 was built to probe the outer reaches of the universe. It did not disappoint. Pioneer 10 was the first nuclear-powered spacecraft, the first to cross the asteroid belt, the first to reach Jupiter, and the first human-made object to leave the solar system. Rendezvousing with Jupiter 20 months after its launch, it provided the richest scientific data ever collected about the planet and returned the first real-time, close-up images. Pioneer 10 reaffirmed TRW's leadership on the frontiers of aerospace technology.

Right: Bolted to the mainframe of Pioneer 10 was this six-inch-by-nine-inch gold-anodized interstellar postcard. Designed by the late astronomer Carl Sagan, the plaque is inscribed with symbols, drawings, and binary numbers to tell any intelligent species about its creators and where they lived.

human resources. This had deep roots reaching back to Fred Crawford and Ray Livingstone in the 1930s. Howard V. Knicely, an outsider from Hart, Schaffner & Marx, took up the post of vice president for human relations in 1979 and saw the challenge of effective human resource management at TRW from the perspective of someone with ties to no particular part of the business. He quickly discerned two sorts of fragmentation bedeviling TRW and, in his judgment, holding it back. The first was the not at all unusual gap that yawned between corporate headquarters and the operating units. The second was the cultural gap that still divided aerospace, with its rocket science heritage, from the historical automotive heart of the company. To bring them together, Knicely believed it was necessary to tie human resource strategy directly to business strategy, and he initiated a broad array of programs to develop employees at all levels and make managers responsible for better performance in the area of human relations.

As if efforts to renew the TRW culture needed a symbol, the company made plans in the early 1980s for a new corporate headquarters complex to be located in Lyndhurst, Ohio, an eastern suburb of Cleveland, on the site of an estate that had once belonged to U.S. Representative Chester Bolton. Bolton and his wife Frances had once been major shareholders of Thompson Products and big supporters of Fred Crawford, so the site had authentic emotional resonance. But the motive for the move was soundly practical: to replace the bursting-at-the-seams facility on the grounds of the old Tapco plant.

The strategic way

The recession of the early 1980s pounded the company's automotive and industrial core, which suffered additionally as Japanese carmakers invaded the North American market with stunning success. TRW's automotive

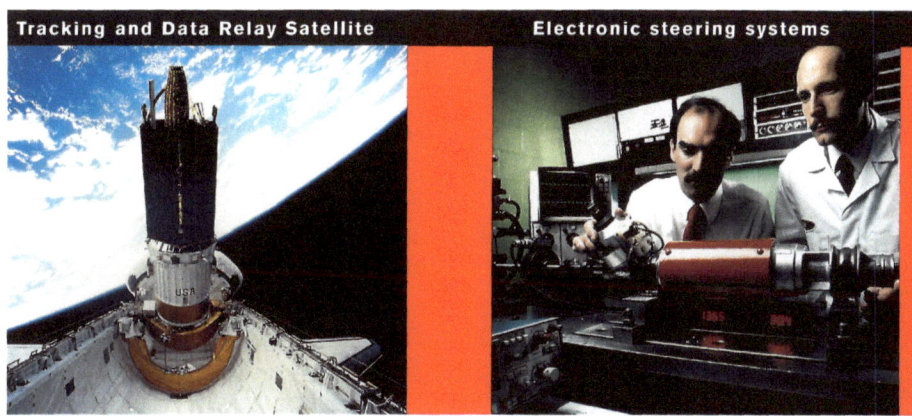

business never lost money, as did many of its customers and competitors in the early 1980s, although sales bobbed disturbingly up and down. With few exceptions, contraction and caution were the watchwords. One promising bright spot was safety products, where German subsidiary Repa was establishing itself as an important supplier to most leading European automakers and was keeping the innovation pipeline full with seat belt products. Careful acquisitions in France, Spain, Italy, and at home combined to make TRW quietly into the leading independent seat belt supplier in the world.

Recession was softened by the Reagan defense boom, which saw Defense Department spending on research and development double in the mid-1980s and propel growth across the broad spectrum of aerospace: ballistic missiles (the Peacekeeper MX ICBMs), high-energy lasers (the Strategic Defense Initiative, "Star Wars"), spacecraft (communications satellites for the Navy and tracking satellites), and all manner of electronic systems and software (the payload for Milstar, the military communications satellite program and the most ambitious space-based communications system in history). Teaming up with Motorola, Space Park scientists pushed the frontier of very high-speed integrated circuitry (VHSIC) that was at the heart of "smart" weapons and in 1983 managed one of the first applications of

Above left: TRW scored a major coup when it became the prime contractor for the Tracking and Data Relay Satellites that provided continuous communications between the earth and objects such as the space shuttle in low-earth orbit. The satellites also freed the United States from dependence on foreign space communication links.

Above right: In the mid-1980s TRW worked to develop electronically controlled, electrically assisted steering systems that could replace power rack and pinion systems.

VHSIC technology in an operational weapons system: the electronic counter-measures of the F-16 fighter. TRW software engineers met their biggest challenge yet with the contract for the ground station that would control NASA's Hubble Space Telescope. But as at earlier junctures, feats of technical derring-do performed for the military and NASA did not spill over to uplift TRW's troubled commercial electronics businesses, and the synergies that Mettler so steadfastly sought seemed as elusive as ever.

Joe Gorman (in the early 1980s getting operating experience as head of the Industrial and Energy sector) not only wondered why this was so but also began to explore new ways to think about TRW's tangle of businesses and to isolate flaws that explained this and other problems. Gorman read management literature deeply and was struck in particular by the work of Harvard Business School Professor Michael Porter on the subject of how companies win, or lose, their competitive advantage. Two factors in Porter's analysis — the structure of the industry a company was in and the position of a company in that industry — determined its competitive performance. Both, in Gorman's judgment, merited some attention at TRW.

The Industrial and Energy sector was the first to feel the discipline of this new form of strategic management. The stress caused by falling oil prices made it a good time systematically to examine strengths and weaknesses in Energy, and the exercise led to some careful retrenchment. On the Industrial side, strategic analysis also came down hard on the bearings and hand tools businesses, where TRW's relative position was not strong and where low-cost imports threatened further decline. Even when bundled with smart technologies from other TRW areas, the business proved balky. And sometimes, as Gorman pointed out, the company had its own shortsightedness to blame. To contain labor costs, in one example, management had decided in the 1970s to relocate an industrial tools plant from Chicago to a nonunion site in Georgia but soon discovered, in high scrap rates and low yields, that something vital had been shed along with the union payroll. "The black magic" possessed by the old workforce was gone, and with it the new plant's competitiveness.

Making the right tactical decisions outside of a coherent strategic vision was hopeless, and a danger that far-flung, decentralized TRW had courted too closely for too long. The Aircraft Components Group, with origins reaching back to World War II defense work, demonstrated the hazards of striving to compete in an industry whose structure increasingly favored buyers, not sellers. In the late 1970s, orders poured in and capacity was expanded at home and abroad, but the cycle ended in 1982, when recession caught up with aircraft sales and with the sales of companies like TRW that supplied the manufacturers. Worse was the problem posed by the shrinking number of those manufacturers, whose power in bargaining for prices rose, even as the uniqueness of TRW's capabilities in this field declined. Cost reduction in such circumstances could be only a palliative.

Gorman became president of TRW in 1985, chairman and chief executive three years later. His commitment to managing the company strategically soon had concrete consequences. He continued to worry, perhaps even more than Stan Pace and Rube Mettler, who promoted him and who sensed the need for a strong strategist at the helm, over the downside of diversification and the disturbing reflex of TRW people to think "more is better." More was better indeed only if the value of the whole exceeded the sum of the parts. The highly charged atmosphere of the times, when scores of once-famous *Fortune*

The growing worldwide energy needs favorably impacted TRW systems for managing oil, gas, and electric power production and distribution, as well as the company's petroleum production systems. One unit to benefit from this growing demand was TRW Reda Pump.

Compton GRO

At 35,000 pounds, NASA's Compton Gamma Ray Observatory (GRO) was the biggest and most complex satellite then placed in orbit. Launched in 1991, it issued a stream of findings that challenged conventional theories about the origins and nature of the universe. Reluctantly, NASA safely performed a controlled deorbit in 2000 of the aging, yet still operational satellite.

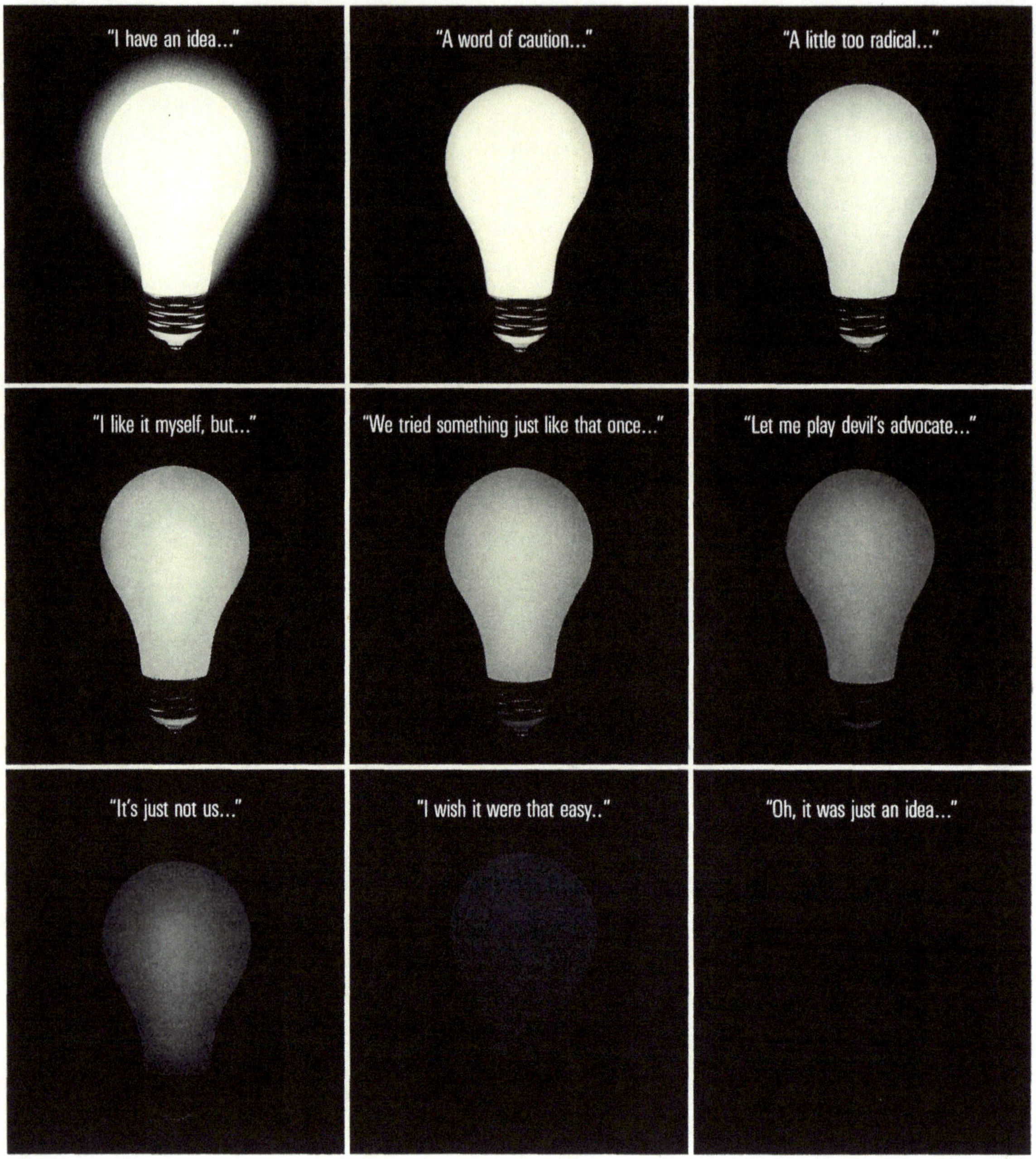

"I have an idea…" "A word of caution…" "A little too radical…"

"I like it myself, but…" "We tried something just like that once…" "Let me play devil's advocate…"

"It's just not us…" "I wish it were that easy.." "Oh, it was just an idea…"

It was just an idea.

An idea is a fragile thing. Turning it off is much easier than keeping it lit.

A company called TRW lives on ideas. So we look for people who have them and for people who won't snuff them out. In recent years TRW has been issued hundreds of patents in such diverse fields as fiber optics, space, lasers and transportation electronics.

Those ideas shone because somebody had them and somebody helped them. And nobody turned them off.

Tomorrow is taking shape at a company called TRW.

A Company Called TRW

© TRW Inc., 1983
TRW is the name and mark of TRW Inc.

500 names were disappearing in hostile takeovers and leveraged buyouts, helped focus everyone's mind on the dangers to highly diversified operations like TRW. How to fend off predators who sniffed big breakup value?

The short answer obviously lay with increasing the value of the whole, but doing so would be painful. Gorman set ambitious financial performance goals aimed at restoring TRW to a strong position among investment peers. Reaching them depended on substantially reducing costs, plus managing strategically in order to get a jump on the future. Division managers across the company got intensive training in the new thinking and were urged, in evaluating their businesses, to focus always on strategies that created the greatest value. This could mean, as it commonly had in the past, acquisitions. It could also mean, as Gorman put it, "major changes in direction, including significant scaling back or restructuring."

The new technique of evaluating the company revealed not only the failure to meet key financial targets, but also areas of activity that held the greatest promise of turning things around. None was more promising than the field of automotive restraint systems, into which TRW had tiptoed with the acquisition of German seat belt manufacturer Repa. New federal regulations, together with changing public sentiment about vehicle safety, were soon to create a lucrative market where none had been before. No other company was more technologically fit to seize it than TRW. But the challenge demanded equal if not greater financial fitness as well. Typically, opportunity costs, and it certainly would cost in this case. Gorman figured the company would need upwards of $1 billion in fresh capital investment.

Pain and gain

TRW's move into its new headquarters coincided symbolically with its move into a new business era. In the autumn of 1985, the company announced a major restructuring, and in doing so it renounced the decades-old tradition of diversification and habits of decentralized management. This was not easy and entailed some painful partings. The biggest was the Aircraft Components Group, which had so buoyed up the company in the early postwar years but where competitive analysis now revealed no future. Along with units of the Electronic Components Group, divestments totaled a hefty $700 million of sales. Putting aside a $170 million reserve to cover the costs of restructuring, the company that year turned in its first annual loss since the 1930s. As the price of oil continued to slump over the next few years, much of TRW's energy businesses also went on the block.

The jolt to the system imposed by Mettler and Gorman's new strategy was healthy medicine taken probably just in time. The morning after, TRW found itself leaner and, management hoped, better able to focus on the three areas that promised greatest growth: automotive supply, space and defense, and information systems and services (the tag given to the credit reporting business).

Perhaps the greatest merit of the new strategic management ideas that Gorman had introduced was their dynamic nature. They banished any single exclusive strategy, such as diversification, and embraced instead a highly pragmatic approach. If exercised skillfully and often — if one really worked at it — they enabled a company, even a big one, to maneuver smartly in changing times.

For TRW, geopolitical revolution that came with the fall of the Soviet Union administered yet another shock to the system, this time

Above: *Forbes* magazine described the TRW of 1983 as "unapologetically conglomerate, unashamedly asset-managed, [and] aggressively multinational as well." The cover story asked, "How unfashionable, and how well managed, can a company possibly get?"

Facing page: For more than a decade, TRW's "light bulb" poster has remained one of the company's most popular ads. Even today, businesses and educators frequently request reprints.

from the outside. The Cold War had demanded furnishing a vast and fearsome arsenal to face down the totalitarians. Because it was "cold" and not "hot," the arsenal thankfully was never used. The missiles that Mettler's technologists had done so much to make ready for reliable launch and accurate delivery deterred but never destroyed their enemy, who in time grew weary and just gave up. But cold or hot, wars mean spending, on which profitable enterprise is built. This was certainly so for TRW, and when the Berlin Wall came tumbling down and "peace was declared," TRW and hundreds of other defense contractors like it faced a sobering future to which past experience held hardly a clue.

Even within Space and Defense, TRW's activities looked safely diversified; in any given year it worked on more than 2,500 different contracts, bench-scale research to projects as big as the Milstar payload. But there was no disguising history's repeating itself, as TRW in the 1980s, much as in the 1950s, had come to rely on defense business for well over half of its revenues. Rebalancing the portfolio came to look doubly urgent, therefore, as shrinking defense and space spending turned up the competitive heat in a market long taken almost for granted. The challenge to Space and Defense sector head Ed Dunford was to concentrate on TRW's strengths in software, lasers, microelectronics, and space technologies and to find business matched to that foundation. This included more work on the Defense Support Program satellites, the Army's worldwide command and control system, and the Navy's ocean surveillance system. As often as not, such projects required teamwork with other firms. Work continued with Honeywell, Hittite Microwave, and General Dynamics on very high-speed integrated circuitry and advanced gallium arsenide microwave technology, to the point where numerous applications suggested themselves, including uses in wireless communications and cellular telephony.

The times called nevertheless for seriously thinning the ranks at Space Park; thus, between 1988 and 1991 employment there fell from 30,000 to 23,000. NASA and other spacecraft customers, just like the military, seemed less and less reliable. In 1990 the national space agency abruptly canceled the Orbiting Maneuvering Vehicle program and later downsized the Advanced X-ray Astrophysics Facility. Such discouragements prompted renewed thinking about ways to apply Space Park technological know-how outside traditional space and defense markets. While Ramo's "civil systems" idea of the 1960s and 1970s had largely come to naught, if it were subjected to the disciplines of strategic management, it was deemed still to hold plausible promise. In pursuit of it, TRW concentrated all of its systems work for the military at a new campus just outside Washington, D.C., and began to look in earnest for new business with the departments of Energy, Interior, and Treasury and with the Federal Aviation Administration.

If the space and defense leg of TRW's business wobbled a bit as a consequence of the "peace dividend" of the early 1990s, it remained in everyone's judgment a business where TRW belonged, without any shadow of a doubt. Managed strategically, investments there could be prudently matched to market opportunities, and TRW's historic technological knowledge base could be preserved and enhanced. The same could not be said, however, for the company's long longed for "third leg," the credit reporting business or, as it was somewhat grandiosely dubbed, "Information Systems." Difficulties in Information Systems accounted for much of the $150 million loss that TRW posted in 1991.

That loss, however, had to be seen in the context of the second major restructuring,

Above: The compact, foldable, two-sided printed circuit board, shown here, was created by TRW in the late '80s for processing signals in avionics systems.

Facing page: The electronics payload aboard the Milstar satellites represented the biggest single contract in TRW's history. The satellites support U.S. defense communications well into the twenty-first century. TRW's ability to win the payload contract partly reflected the company's unsurpassed capabilities in microelectronics in the late '70s.

which Gorman wrought on the company that year. Credit reporting clearly was failing the tests of strategic management, and TRW's leaders shortly concluded that this was a business not for them and decided to exit as soon as the unit could be restored to salable health (which took time and was accomplished in 1996 for consideration of approximately $1 billion). "Four percent of our sales," as Gorman put it, did not justify "a third of our headaches."

The restructuring, of which that sale was the final act, raised TRW to the new level of strategic fitness that turbulent times required. As in the previous restructuring in 1985, the pain was distributed widely. The sector layer of management disappeared. Space and defense was reorganized into two groups related to their markets: Space & Electronics, which stayed in Space Park; and the Systems Integration Group, which already had moved to northern Virginia near Washington, D.C. On the automotive side, a gradual reorganization left four entities reporting directly to the top: Occupant Restraints & Controls, Steering Systems, Controls & Fasteners, and Engine Components. Company-wide divestitures would approach $500 million. Capital spending would fall $100 million. Twenty-five hundred employees would go.

Safety bet

Restructurings can be scary, but TRW's two restructurings in barely half a dozen years yielded a renaissance. Fred Crawford, who lived to be 103 and witnessed both, could well have smiled with satisfaction. For sure, he hadn't had all the answers. TRW turned out not to need a "third leg" after all. But Crawford had guessed right about tying up a bunch of Cleveland metal benders with some California eggheads in the hope that something profitable would come of it. And of course he had been right in sticking, at the same time, to the business that the old Thompson Products had been in when he had first showed up for work there back in 1916. Joe Gorman's biggest bet of all confirmed, once again, that it was a very good business still to be in.

America's fascination with the magic of automotive transportation — freedom, convenience, speed — had diminished not a whit in a hundred years. Indeed, it had become vastly more democratic, and at the end of the twentieth century, a truly global enthusiasm. Everyone envied roads like America's, and while it was said by some that Japanese cars for a time were better than American ones, the "national origins" of cars and trucks were anyway getting harder and harder to distinguish and mattered less and less to the people who drove them. What they wanted was reliability, economy, and safety.

The components that TP and then TRW had made for years, from engine valves to steering mechanisms, had redefined upward accepted standards of reliability. Economy came with the lighter vehicles and more efficient engines that were the result of federally mandated fuel mileage standards, themselves a political response to successive oil shocks and fears about exhaust emissions and air pollution. Safety came with regulation too, and TRW was well prepared to build a new business on

Credit reporting

By the mid-1980s, TRW's consumer credit database had swelled to profiles of 140 million individuals. Information systems and services revenues peaked in 1989 at $705 million. But by 1996 the company decided that the business was no longer core, and the unit was sold.

Internationale Automobil-Ausstellung

Simply the most important automotive trade show in Europe, the Internationale Automobil-Ausstellung, held every two years in Frankfurt, Germany, is the destination of decision-makers in the auto manufacturing and supply business.

During the two-week show, TRW showcases a variety of products and systems in its major lines of braking systems, vehicle dynamics control systems, electronic systems, and occupant safety systems.

The company's booth usually features live narration and is among the show's most popular.

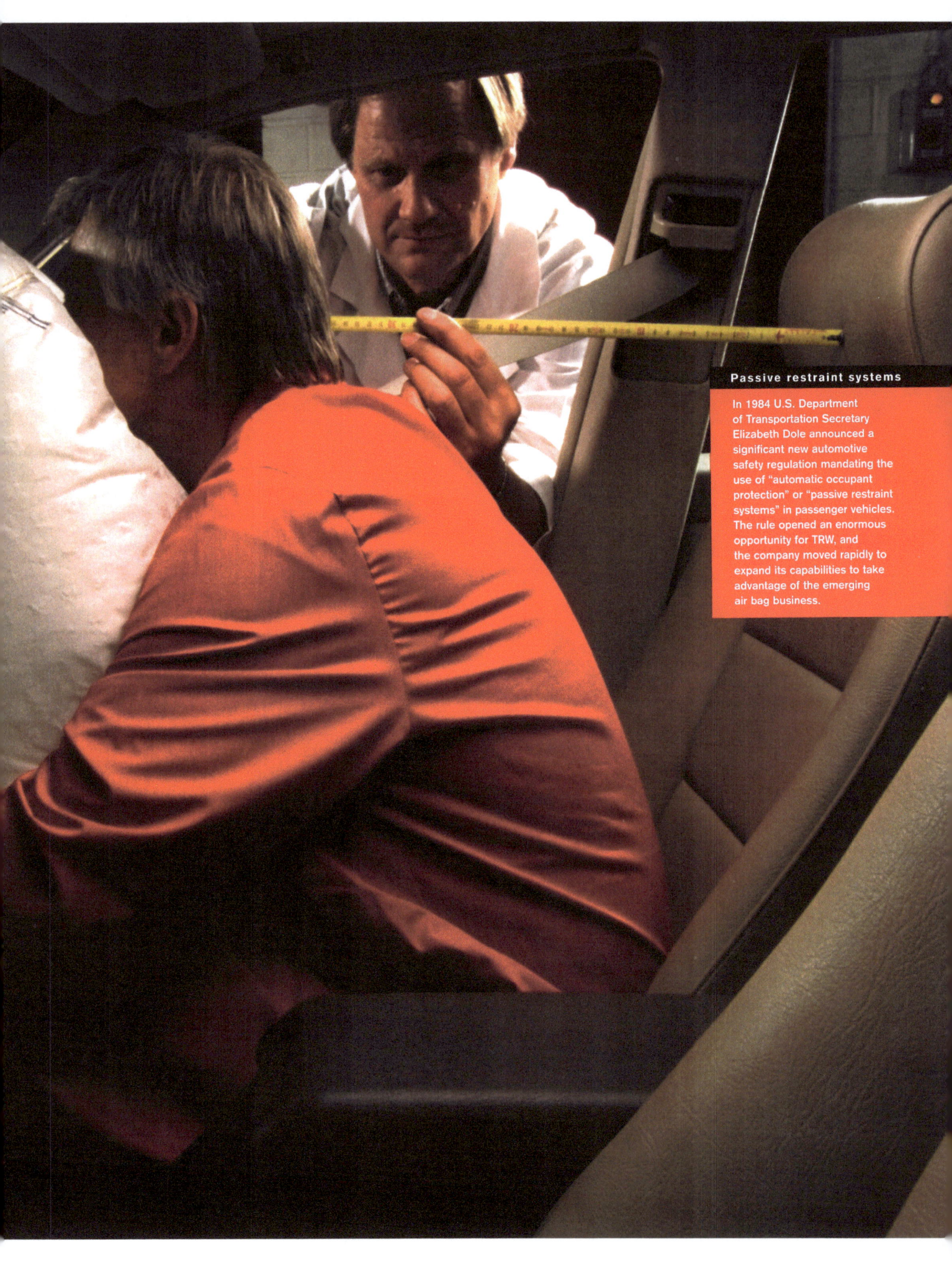

Passive restraint systems

In 1984 U.S. Department of Transportation Secretary Elizabeth Dole announced a significant new automotive safety regulation mandating the use of "automatic occupant protection" or "passive restraint systems" in passenger vehicles. The rule opened an enormous opportunity for TRW, and the company moved rapidly to expand its capabilities to take advantage of the emerging air bag business.

it. The watershed regulation, known as Federal Motor Vehicle Safety Standard Number 208, came down from the U.S. Department of Transportation in 1984 and dictated use of automatic occupant protection, or passive restraint systems in passenger vehicles, to be phased in starting with the 1987 model year. For TRW, which in 1984 acquired Firestone's seat belt business and already had a leading position in seat belt technology, the new mandate opened an enormous opportunity.

Senior management envisioned TRW's automotive business as similar, but different, from what it had been in the past. Perceiving major changes under way in the world auto industry, they determined to make TRW a closely linked first-tier supplier to automakers in North America, Europe, and Asia and no longer a supplier of just parts and components, but of modules and systems. As they quickly evolved, occupant restraint systems presented complex technical challenges and were the test of that vision.

The law stipulated no particular technology, and TRW's expertise with seat belts proved only the beginning. While several leading automakers and suppliers had fiddled with air bags during the 1970s, none had had much success, and high costs had kept the systems out of all but luxury models. The challenge to master the new technology and bring it to the mass market promised to be expensive but also highly rewarding. It adapted naturally to the systems approaches that TRW had pioneered and honed so well in its space and defense work. With remarkable speed, the capabilities of Repa and the operations acquired from Firestone were combined with insights from the aerospace side of the business into electronic sensing, pyrotechnics, and propellants to build a new technology. One careful acquisition (of California-based sensor supplier Technar) and one joint venture (with Imperial Chemical Industries for manufacture of the gas generant for passenger-side air bags) gave TRW capabilities in all key air bag technologies that no other supplier could boast.

TRW marketed its technology aggressively and soon won a breakthrough agreement with Ford to become sole supplier of its occupant restraint systems in North America. Other deals soon followed with Chrysler and GM, and even with Japanese carmakers to supply virtually all of their North American requirements. Charles L. Miller, whom Gorman made head of a dedicated restraint systems business unit in 1987, projected the market's doubling in five years.

Engineered fasteners

To satisfy it, TRW acquired its own chief supplier of driver-side modules (Talley) two years later and, with it, a key manufacturing facility in Mesa, Arizona. The total effort, from mastering the technology to ramping up the production, consumed enormous sums. It also returned enormous dividends and positioned TRW for global leadership in automotive supply.

Automotive supply is where everything began. It is not where everything ends. If cars were to be mandated out of existence tomorrow (as occupant restraints were mandated in), it is fair to imagine TRW carrying on capably in some other, perhaps today entirely unthought of, line of business. This is one measure of a company that has used its history well. Things change, and all markets change too. Major strategic moves late in the 1990s would suggest how TRW proposed changing to meet them.

Above left: TRW entered the fasteners business in 1967 with the purchase of United-Carr. The deal came about largely because Crawford was a friend of Sinclair Weeks, who founded United-Carr in 1929 through the merger of two Boston-based fastener makers. Today, TRW provides the automotive industry with more than 6 billion fasteners annually, including interior components, temperature control systems, air pressure relief valves, and precision plastic moldings and assemblies.

Above right: The fasteners business also has teamed with TRW's electronics business to design and produce specialty molded products, such as the overhead console shown here.

1999–2001

6

Adding up and building out

Left: Media interest was intense when TRW announced its acquisition of LucasVarity on January 28, 1999. At a press conference in New York City, Gorman answered questions about the $7 billion purchase. He has said of the deal, "There is no combination of two automotive companies in the world that provides as much synergy."

Above: With the purchase of LucasVarity, TRW acquired a company whose roots exceeded even its own. Lucas, in fact, was established in 1875 in Birmingham, England, as a maker of ship lamps and began supplying Europe's infant automotive industry four years later. A 1996 merger with Varity Corp. created LucasVarity.

Facing page: In 1968 Indiana native and Yale Law School graduate Joseph Tolle Gorman joined TRW after gaining experience at a leading Cleveland law firm. Rising quickly through the ranks, he was just 51 years old when he was named chairman and CEO in 1988. Gorman has said of TRW, "We have a vast storehouse of technological expertise in this company."

Joe Gorman is TRW's longest-serving chairman after Fred Crawford, and when the history of TRW in the first decade or two of the twenty-first century is written, that account will probably conclude that the two leaders had much else in common. History never repeats itself exactly, though sometimes, as Mark Twain once said, it rhymes. Between Crawford's bold move in the 1950s to join forces with Simon Ramo and Dean Wooldridge and position his nuts-and-bolts manufacturing company for growth in the then-dawning space age, and Gorman's moves in the late 1990s to fit out TRW for profitable growth in the globally competitive and changing-overnight automotive, aerospace, and defense industries, there were distinct parallels. Like Crawford, Gorman had spent virtually his entire career at TRW, and he learned respect for its hardiness and resilience, its ability to go the distance. The story of all businesses is a record of gradual evolution, of building on past successes and learning from mistakes. When Gorman characterized TRW as "running a marathon, not the 100-yard dash," a nearly 100-year history of building and learning backed him up.

TRW's disciplined restructurings of the 1980s and early 1990s yielded sustained high financial performance, which gave the company the luxury of some options, looking ahead. Gorman's executive team framed the company's future in terms of two broad-bore/what-next questions. One: What do we do next in automotive? Two: How do we move into new dimensions in space, defense, and information systems? The answers had begun to emerge in the mid-1980s when TRW bought key air bag technologies and in the early 1990s when it developed its own air bag production, which, when merged with its seat belt capabilities and using the steering gear business as an anchor, foreshadowed a powerful new focus on automotive safety. Starting in 1996, three major acquisitions further filled in the picture.

Shortly before the end of 1996, TRW announced formation of a strategic alliance with Magna International, a $5 billion automotive supplier based in Canada. The transaction bolstered TRW's strategy for the design, development, and production of automotive safety products for the global market. Magna was one of the most diversified automotive suppliers in the world, with 120 manufacturing operations in 11 countries and products that included vehicle body-in-white superstructures, exterior decorative systems, stamped and welded metal parts and assemblies, seating systems, and instrument panels. TRW's chief interest, however, focused on two particular Magna-owned operations: MST Automotive GmbH Automobil-Sicherheitstechnik, a European supplier of air bag modules, steering wheels, and other related automotive components; and Temic Bayern-Chemie Airbag GmbH, a supplier of air bag inflators and propellants. The move dramatically enhanced TRW's position as a world leader in occupant safety and enhanced its leadership position in developing advanced interior and safety systems for global-scale markets. The Magna alliance also had a second part: development in Germany of a joint TRW-Magna technical research center whose work would directly address systems-oriented design challenges and consumer demands for integrated restraints and vehicle structure.

The idea was to form teams focusing on total vehicle safety systems integration, and it was an idea rooted in a historic TRW strength. Back in the 1950s, Ramo and Wooldridge had brought the principle of "the systems approach" to TRW's management of the Air Force's early intercontinental ballistic missile (ICBM) program, from whence it spread to engineering schools and leading technology companies around the world. The "systems approach," as Ramo has explained it for more than 40 years, "is an intellectual discipline for mobilizing science and technology to attack complex, large-scale problems in an objective, complete, and thoroughly professional manner." Increasingly, automobiles as much as ICBMs are coming to consist not just of parts bolted together, but of a number of technologically sophisticated and highly integrated systems: engine management, steering and suspension, transmission, braking and traction, safety and convenience. Already, TRW had positioned itself to lead in this conceptual shift in the automotive industry by having established the Center for Automotive Technology (CAT), located at Space Park on the West Coast. In the CAT, TRW Automotive employees were involved with aerospace and defense engineers in efforts to transfer aerospace technology into Automotive's development and production of modern automobile systems. Their work accelerated the evolution of smart restraint technologies and, in particular, air bag propellant technology.

One year after announcement of the Magna alliance, TRW closed its biggest acquisition to date: an all-cash tender offer valued at

A 1996 partnership with Magna International was heralded by Gorman as "one of TRW's most exciting alliances ever." The agreement called for TRW to purchase 80 percent of two European operations held by Magna and to jointly establish a technical center. Those operations, now wholly owned by TRW, employed 2,500 in Germany, Spain, and the Czech Republic in the production of air bag inflators and propellants (above) as well as air bag modules and steering wheels (facing page).

Fingerprint identification

State, local, and international governments are using technology developed by TRW Systems & Information Technology Group, based in Reston, Virginia, to fight crime. A TRW-designed fingerprint identification system can identify and track criminals and connect police forces to a single site.

$1 billion for BDM International, Inc. (BDM). Based in McLean, Virginia, near Washington, D.C., BDM was a fast-growing multinational information technology company and a recognized world leader in providing systems integration and computer services to the defense industry and government entities, as well as to private companies. BDM was no stranger to ambitious projects, having designed EDGAR, the electronic filing system used by the Securities and Exchange Commission. The merger of BDM into TRW brought together two advanced-technology companies with similar cultures and backgrounds dating back to the 1950s, and with the same aims in the late 1990s of increasing nondefense-related business. Although they were in similar businesses, TRW and BDM were truly complementary organizations with little or no overlap. TRW marketed, for instance, a fingerprinting system for the criminal-justice system while BDM sold a police system that handled arrests and bookings. Similarly on the automotive side, TRW was a leading supplier of steering gears and air bags while BDM sold a product that helped automotive companies more efficiently manage their warehouses and inventories.

The merger advanced at once several important corporate goals. It expanded the reach and scope of TRW's space and defense business. It reinforced existing systems integration and information technology businesses. And it broadened TRW's offerings of services and products to government customers while increasing its participation in growing civil and commercial markets. Moreover, BDM had operations in the Middle East and a strong position in Europe that bolstered TRW's presence in the European Union. The merger positioned the enlarged TRW for further international growth and was, up to then, the most significant single leap forward in a long-term strategy to double the company's size every seven years.

As the new millennium approached, which would also mark the beginning of TRW's second century, the automotive industry found itself undergoing fundamental structural change unlike anything seen since the first large car companies were put together decades ago. Global markets, corporate consolidation, price pressures, and insistent quality demands created a bracing competitive environment that winnowed once-comfortable and confident organizations. Many of the world's automakers found themselves losing money and saddled with overcapacity. Consumers wanted safer, more efficient vehicles but also wanted to pay less for them. Regulatory mandates for cleaner burning low-emission engines meant development costs that were hard to spread out when too few vehicles were being sold. Suppliers, in turn, also found themselves squeezed to cut costs, raise quality, absorb engineering costs, and deliver ever higher value to the manufacturers.

In this context, TRW set forth into a decisive next chapter of automotive history with its third and largest acquisition in less than five years, announcing early in 1999 its purchase for $7 billion in cash of British auto and aerospace parts maker LucasVarity plc. The move signaled an offensive thrust on the part of TRW's Gorman as bold as any in the company's history since Fred Crawford's bet nearly half a century earlier on the vision of rocket scientists Ramo and Wooldridge. Gorman's move came at a time fraught with corporate mergers, many much larger than this. But within its industry, the TRW/LucasVarity combination ranked among the most significant. It acknowledged the pervasive consolidation of industrial suppliers and secured TRW's place, with continuing revenues of $11 billion in automotive supply, among the top tier-one players in the business. The merger gave TRW the critical mass and systems capabilities to compete with the other global independents

Acquisitions

The acquisitions of BDM, for $1 billion in 1997, and LucasVarity, for $7 billion in 1999, each represented TRW's largest purchase to date and underscored the company's philosophy to be a leader in the markets it serves.

Advanced Car Technology Systems center

and with giant industry "insiders," once captive to the big manufacturers but themselves becoming increasingly independent. LucasVarity added braking and electronics capabilities to TRW's portfolio, along with strong emerging market positions in China and India.

TRW Automotive accounted for more than 60 percent of the company's combined revenues, and in order to grow faster than the industry, TRW needed to find ways to engage the competition on many fronts simultaneously. As manufacturers grew more reliant on suppliers for design and engineering tasks, TRW prepared to capitalize on its strengths in occupant safety systems, electronics, and steering and suspension systems. This could be seen in the rising value of TRW content in new vehicles. In 1998 a new Jeep Cherokee contained $217 worth of TRW parts and systems. Two years later that number had jumped to more than $1,000. By adding LucasVarity's braking capability — it was the world's second largest brake manufacturer — to its existing strengths, TRW stood to secure a uniquely powerful position as supplier not just of more and more components, but of the interrelated and increasingly modular electronics-controlled systems that pointed the way toward new technologies like Integrated Vehicle Control Systems.

Good technological fit underscored the strategic congruence of the new partnership as an instrument to achieve enhanced financial performance. Both firms already had learned on their own what it meant to be low-cost producers and how to strike the balance that, according to Gorman, would enable suppliers like TRW and the original equipment makers to profit in the long haul. The text of this new chapter will be written in the years to come, but it was clear at the outset that the highly complementary capabilities of the two firms promised to yield classic benefits from consolidation. LucasVarity's historic stature as a leading European corporation, in addition, made the combined entity much more global, with greater reach into all three major automotive markets: North America, Europe, and Asia.

No strategy is more effective, however, than the leadership that must drive it forward, day by day. With the influence of the financial market's "scorecard" mentality growing, Gorman knew TRW needed a strong second-in-command. What he had in mind was an executive with the reputation, accomplishments, and leadership skills to instill confidence in company stakeholders. He began a year-long search of the global business talent pool, seeking someone with the professional skills and personal attributes necessary to lead TRW into the global information economy.

Not surprisingly, his search took him to highly admired General Electric, where David M. Cote, a 25-year veteran of the company, was at the helm of GE Appliances.

TRW in November 1999 selected Cote as its new president and chief operating officer, and his immediate task was to focus total attention on TRW's expanded automotive supply business.

Cote was well acquainted with lean manufacturing and high-volume production and was experienced in managing complex global businesses under challenging market conditions. He believed that sustained superior performance depended on having in place the very best processes in operations, strategy, and human resources. Galvanizing everyone to a best-practice focus, he wasted no time in broadcasting across the company a renewed call to arms. He wanted the best people, and he wanted them to behave as if the company were engaged "in a war to obtain the highest quality, lowest price products and services to support our customers." Details mattered, from vigilance over quality, delivery, and supplier costs that could make or break the

In June 1999 TRW and Magna International opened the joint $33 million Advanced Car Technology Systems (ACTS) center in Sailauf, Germany. The venture is among the world's most advanced independent centers for development of modular, functional, and safety systems.

Inset: ACTS also features areas for testing, such as this simulation of a rollover accident.

company every day, to nurturing entrepreneurial ideas that awaited transformation into products and services customers wanted to buy.

The same year, 1999, not only was the automotive industry restructuring and forcing radical new disciplines on all players, but the aerospace and information systems industry also was moving into its own new era characterized, above all, by the ubiquity of communication and the accessibility of information. In this fast-changing context, TRW accelerated its quest for new opportunities in space, defense, and information systems businesses.

An extra benefit of the LucasVarity acquisition was Lucas Aerospace, a supplier to the global aerospace industry of high-integrity systems in engine controls, flight controls, and power generation and management. Its integration into TRW Aerospace & Information Systems (A&IS) was an early immediate goal and part of TRW's ongoing strategic assessment of markets and opportunities. Lucas Aerospace (renamed Aeronautical Systems Group) plus TRW's Space & Electronics Group and Systems & Information Technology Group formed a diverse, technology-rich set of enterprises ready for new challenges. And as with the automotive side, the LucasVarity addition made TRW A&IS a truly transatlantic aerospace and defense business. With that new reach, the A&IS team focused on several areas to win profitable growth.

In TRW's traditional military and intelligence markets, the plan was to concentrate on programs capitalizing on the need for and the ability to deliver information superiority. With the conduct of warfare changing from old doctrines of confrontation between vast armored land forces to strategies demanding increasingly "smart" stand-off weaponry and technologies delivering mission superiority on the electronic battlefield, A&IS responded

with an array of evolving capabilities under the umbrella concept of "C4ISR," which stood for command, control, communications, computers, intelligence, surveillance, and reconnaissance. Another important area of growth is use of information technology to enhance the armed forces' combat readiness through improved training and the simulation of the widest range of battle contingencies.

TRW also carried on in the vital national security role begun nearly half a century ago: managing for the Air Force the country's ICBM program. Simultaneously, the company advanced breakthrough technologies in three regimes of high-energy laser defense against incoming missiles: the airborne laser, to be carried aboard a modified Boeing 747 aircraft and designed to shoot down theater weapons launched hundreds of miles away; the tactical high-energy laser, a joint U.S.-Israeli effort designed to protect troops in the field; and the space-based laser.

In civilian aerospace and information businesses, TRW notched up a series of technological triumphs and expanded its universe of satisfied customers. It delivered to NASA the Chandra X-ray Observatory, which was launched on the Space Shuttle Columbia in 1999 and activated flawlessly. Chandra was the third in NASA's family of "Great Observatories," which included the Compton Gamma Ray Observatory, also built by TRW. A triumph of systems management, Chandra was 45 feet tall, weighed five tons, and carried the world's largest X-ray telescope as well as high-resolution imaging and spectroscopy instruments. It was also an example of how TRW has mastered the processes needed to build the tools that will advance basic scientific research. TRW is also building the digital communications payload for the Astrolink satellites, a wireless broadband satellite joint venture of TRW, Lockheed Martin, Telecom Italia, and Liberty Media Group. The prospect

Above: As the prime hardware and software contractor for the Force XXI Battle Command Brigade and Below (FBCB2), TRW is helping implement techniques that will take the Army command-and-control into the twenty-first century.

Facing page: A TRW-led team designed and built NASA's Chandra X-ray Observatory, named for the late Indian-American Nobel Laureate and twentieth century astrophysicist Subrahmanyan Chandrasekhar. The five-ton, 45-foot-tall satellite views cosmic objects in the X-ray portion of the spectrum and has captured awards from *Popular Science* and *Discover* magazines.

of ever faster broadband telecommunications systems advanced with TRW's demonstration of the world's fastest digital integrated circuit made out of indium phosphide, which operates at 69 gigahertz. And the Year 2000 United States Census went forward with help from TRW, which with partners operated the data centers that processed 120 million questionnaires. It was the first time that the government had outsourced processing in the 200-year history of the census.

While maintaining leadership in core programs, A&IS managers and engineers also pushed themselves to spawn new businesses with high potential to create value far into the future. This "technology bank" was a corporate treasure trove waiting to be unlocked and applied according to a new model in which TRW would take the best of what it did, which was technology, affiliate with a commercial enterprise that knows the market, and then take a significant but not necessarily controlling position in the new enterprise. The equity potential of this approach soon became clear, with analysts ascribing as much as $20 of the company's share price to such ventures. Astrolink was an example of a TRW core technology applied in this way, as was RF Micro Devices, which made wireless communication amplifier chips with TRW's gallium arsenide technology.

By midyear 2000 the technology bank accounted for 11 ventures. The company was witnessing a unique convergence of opportunity between its space and defense core competencies and the explosive marketplace for the Internet and telecommunications. A sequence of value-creating commercial ventures ensued, capitalizing on TRW's core technology strengths in wideband wireless communications, lasers, advanced microelectronics, and information technology. Noncore TRW technologies also were licensed and transferred to strategic partners who created ventures such as, in two early examples, E-Sync Networks, which used TRW technology for electronic message transmission and networking, and E-Certify, which applied TRW technology to achieve secure computer-to-computer, business-to-business communications. Such ventures would also profit from their affinity with TRW's long tradition of "systems" thinking: connecting many complex processes into working systems and making them function quicker and more efficiently. The ability to solve tough technological problems, Gorman noted, was something the company had nurtured since the 1930s, and it still remains a key strength.

Conversations with Gorman and Cote on the eve of the company's 100th anniversary reveal an unabashed confidence that, with the right management team now in place, TRW stands poised for a new chapter in its history. Exciting for its "no one has ever done this before" newness, it will also be a chapter built on a long and solid tradition of applying technological prowess in the service of superior financial performance.

Cote quickly became the driving force behind the company's plunge into the newly emerging e-business economy. As the Internet revolution swept through the business world, Cote set the vision for TRW. "E-business can help us eliminate bureaucracy and improve speed. It can be the glue that holds all of TRW together," he proclaimed. To demonstrate his commitment, he formed an organization dedicated to the development and implementation of a corporate e-business strategy. "Our goal is to see to it that e-business becomes embedded in all aspects of our internal and external processes."

"We're the best in the world at much of what we do, literally," says Gorman. "And that's important." It is important because the business and technology landscapes are changing so fast as to make any of his predecessors' heads spin.

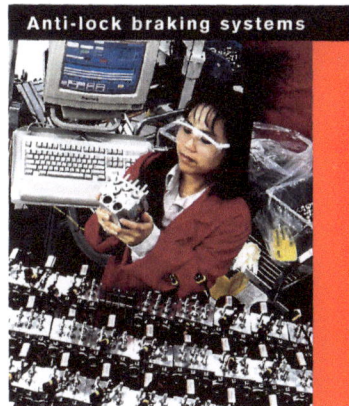

Above: With the purchase of LucasVarity, TRW became the world's second-largest braking supplier and North America's No. 1 maker of anti-lock braking systems (ABS). Employees made history when, in early 1999, they produced their 50 millionth ABS unit.

Facing page: David M. Cote joined TRW in late 1999 as president and chief operating officer and was charged with overseeing the company's automotive businesses. He traveled to Thailand in July 2000 to attend the grand opening of a manufacturing facility in Rayong. The chassis systems plant supplies components and actuation systems to General Motors.

"Best" today, however, assures nothing tomorrow, and the future promises only to be filled with unforgiving competitive challenges. How to turn those challenges into opportunities and to profit from them through superior service to customers are unrelenting daily tasks, from the office of the chief executive to the front line at every TRW laboratory and manufacturing facility around the world. They are ambitious tasks, and there is no false humility when Gorman adds that "we're trying to find the right path in all of this."

TRW has become a multi-industry company whose people are its most important capital asset. Managing them, motivating them, and keeping their talents replenished and recharged for TRW will be among leadership's biggest challenges in the years ahead. Another challenge will be strategic and will demand decisions about how best to pursue profitable growth in the future and create value for shareholders. Several options suggest themselves, alone or in combination. The company might continue to configure itself as a two-industry multi-industry company. It might pursue further acquisitions to create a three- or four- or more-industry company. It might rely on its own considerable regenerative capabilities to grow new industries from the inside. In this, understanding the history of years past will help. For TRW has met and mastered strategic challenges before and has learned some fundamentals along the way. Future longevity and prosperity will require looking ahead and also looking back.

TRW's story thus far has been the story of meeting change head on while polishing assets built up over long decades of hard work at high risk. The company began with making cap screws and then engine valves. Today it makes anti-lock brakes, dual-stage air bags, satellites and payloads, plus much more. But the source of TRW's strength today and tomorrow — this is history's chief lesson — lies less with any particular product than with a store of special capabilities in technology, manufacturing, and management.

As future company leaders peer ahead, history will tell them something of the principles that have worked before, across different times and in changing circumstances, to sustain growth and competitiveness. Technological innovation, they will be reminded, means attracting and nurturing the best human capital, which is always expensive and always requires patience. Openness to fresh opportunities and the willingness to rework the organization to capture them, they will learn from the merger of TP and R-W and the restructurings and acquisitions of the 1980s and 1990s, can produce powerful transformation and renewal. Enlightened human relations, Crawford's example will tell them, are inseparable from lasting wealth creation. And from the record of smooth successions and long-serving leaders, they will take home the lesson that everything depends on steadfastness and resolution at the top.

Airborne laser

Indium phosphide

Left: TRW is part of a team under contract to the U.S. Air Force to develop, build, and flight test the first prototype airborne laser (ABL). The ABL weapon system uses a high-energy chemical oxygen iodine laser mounted on a modified 747 to shoot down theater ballistic missiles in their boost phase.

Above: In the 1980s TRW worked to develop semiconductors made of gallium arsenide (GaAs) for satellites. By the late 1990s GaAs chips were being used commercially in radios and cell phones. As the twenty-first century begins, TRW is making faster, more efficient devices from indium phosphide for use in the next generation of fiber optic and wireless broadband systems.

Index

Able rocket, 67

A-bomb, 62

Acquisitions by Electric Welding Products, 15

Acquisitions by Thompson Products, 37, 67–69

Acquisitions by TRW, 80, 82, 85–88, 91, 99, 103, 109, 111–112, 115, 118, 122. *See also* Joint ventures of TRW

Advanced Car Technology Systems (ACTS) center, 117

Advanced X-ray Astrophysics Facility, 105

Advertisements of Thompson Products, 22, 29, 34, 37–38, 54

Advertisements of TRW, 82, 91–92, 97, 103

Aeronautical Systems Group, 118

Aerospace Corporation, 74–75, 77
See also Space Technology Laboratories

Aerospace & Information Systems (A&IS) of TRW, 118, 121

Aerospace technology
Space Technology Laboratories in, 74–75, 77
TRW restructuring developments in, 105, 112, 115, 118
See also Missile programs; Satellite technology

African-Americans, World War II workforce of, 54–55

Age of affluence, 71

Air bags, 103, 108–109, 112, 115, 122. *See also* Automotive restraint systems

Air Force, 59, 94, 118, 123
in partnership with Space Technology Laboratories, 72–74, 77, 79
Ramo-Wooldridge developments with, 61–62, 64–65, 67, 112
Tapco developments with, 53
Western Development Command of, 64

Aircraft Components Group of TRW, 100, 103

Aircraft industry, 38
commercial opportunities, 88
growth of, 20
manufacturing of valves in, 17, 20, 22, 24, 29
Thompson Products business pre-World War II in, 33–34, 38
Thompson Products post-World War II business in, 59–60
Thompson Products World War II business in, 50, 53

Aircraft parts
post-World War II, 59–61, 81, 88, 100
pre-World War II, 31, 33–34, 38
World War II, 50, 53–54, 59
See also Valves, aircraft engines

Aldrin, Buzz, 71

Alloys, 15, 17, 34

American Federation of Labor, 44

Antiballistic missiles, 91

Antitrust legislation, 80

Apollo missions, 22, 79, 90–93

Armstrong, Neil, 71

Armstrong, Percival, 17–18

Army, 49, 105, 118

Army Air Corps, 20, 22

Army-Navy E award, 49–50

Astrolink satellites, 118, 121

Atlas missiles, 62, 64, 67, 72

Automobile industry
acquisitions in, 15, 37, 80, 86–87, 91, 99, 103, 109, 112, 115, 117
mass production in, 13
Big Three in, 27, 29, 87
post-World War II boom in, 56, 59
replacement market in, 20, 33–34, 36–38, 59, 80, 87
rise of, 9–10, 106
use of silcrome valves in, 17–18, 20, 34, 37

Automotive Group of TRW, 80, 85, 117

Automotive Hall of Fame, 31

Automotive International Division of TRW, 86–87

Automotive original equipment, 33–34, 36, 38, 87

Automotive parts, standardized, 12, 27

Automotive replacement parts, 20, 33–34, 36–38, 59, 80, 87

Automotive safety systems, 95, 103, 106–109, 112, 117, 122
See also Air bags; Seat belts; Steering wheels

BDM International, Inc., 112, 115

Ball joint suspension, 59, 87

Bartlett, William (Billy) D., 12, 15, 27

Bayles, Lowell, 26

Bearings, 80, 100

Bement, Arden, 97

Big Three automakers, 27, 29, 87
See also Chrysler; Ford; General Motors

Bissell, Dick, 17

Blitzkrieg, 50

Bolton, Chester, 97, 99

Bolton, Frances, 97, 99

Braking systems, 107, 112, 117, 121–122

Brelsford, Ernie, 82

Bright, Frederick E., 7, 9

Bright, H. Verner, 7, 9

Broadband telecommunications systems, 118, 121, 123

Bubb, Harry, 33, 54

Buick, 20

Bunker-Ramo Corporation, 80

Bureau of Aeronautics, 17

Burgin, Bob, 87

Business Week, 54, 67, 85

C4ISR, 118

Cam Gears Ltd., 91

Cape Canaveral, 65

Cape Codizing, 59

Cap screws, 7, 9–10, 122

Carbon-arc lighting system, 77

Carr, William F., 7

Cellular telephony, 105, 123

Census 2000, 121

Center for Automotive Technology (CAT), 112

Chandra X-ray Observatory, 118

Chandrasekhar, Subrahmanyan, 118

Chassis parts and systems, 80, 87, 121

Chateau Gloria, 27

Chevrolet, 34, 37, 53–54

Chrysler, 27, 34, 109. *See also* Big Three automakers

Circuit boards, 105

Civil Systems, 105

Clarkwood Road plant, 7, 12, 14, 50

Clegg, Lee, 22, 25, 54, 57

Cleveland Cap Screw Company
Articles of Incorporation of, 7
creation of, 5, 7, 94
manufacturing of auto engine valves at, 9–10
promotional literature for, 7
sale of, 8–9

Cleveland Plain Dealer, 54

Cold War, 44, 64, 72, 79, 105

Columbia Space Shuttle, 118

Colwell, Arch, 33–34, 38, 49, 54, 57, 62, 82

Command and control systems, 105, 118

"Company called TRW, A" slogan, 97

Compressors, aircraft, 54

Compton Gamma Ray Observatory (GRO), 101, 118

Computer services, 80, 91, 115

Congress of Industrial Organizations (CIO), 47, 53, 56

Conn, Henry, 97

Controls & Fasteners Group of TRW, 106

Control systems, 82, 109, 112, 118

Coolidge, Jim, 54, 57

Cote, David (Dave) M., 117, 121

Crawford, Frederick (Fred) Coolidge, 12, 19, 25, 31, 94, 99, 111, 115
business and management qualities of, 25, 31, 33–34, 38, 71, 79–80, 88, 106, 122
on Charlie Thompson, 15, 27
on labor relations, 41–45, 47, 54, 56–57, 97
education and beginnings at Steel Products, 17–18, 20
leadership during World War II, 49–50, 53–54, 56, 67
post-World War II developments of, 56, 59, 61
Triangle of Plenty, 18, 42, 44

Credit Data Corporation, 85

Credit reporting, 85, 103, 105–106

Curtis, William H., 53

Curtiss-Wright, 25, 27

Data processing, 85, 91
See also Information technology

Davis, Doug, 25, 27

Dean, Hugh, 54

Decentralization, 59, 97, 103

Defense business, 100, 105, 118
See also Electronics, defense

Defense Department, 59, 64, 72, 99. *See also* Pentagon

Defense Plant Corporation, 50

Defense Support Program, 105

DeLauer, Richard D., 77

124

Depression. *See* Great Depression
Devil's steel, 17
Discover, 118
Diversification, 61, 80, 82, 85, 88, 91, 93–94, 97, 100, 103, 105, 112
Dodge, 20, 37
Dole, Elizabeth, 108
Doll, Edward B., 77
Donovan, Al, 74
Doolittle, Jimmy, 26
Duggan, Tom, 33, 36–37
Dunford, Edsel (Ed) D., 105
Dunn, Louis, 67
DuPont, 59, 87

EDGAR, 115
E award, 49–50
E-business, 121
E-Certify, 121
E-Sync Networks, 121
Earhart, Amelia, 38
Ehrenreich & Cie., 86–87
Eisenhower, Dwight, 59, 64, 67, 72
Electric Welding Products Company, 9–10, 12–13, 15
Electronics and Defense sector of TRW, 97
Electronic Components Group of TRW, 82, 97, 103
Electronics industry, 91
   automotive, 107, 109, 112, 117
   commercial, 67, 79–80, 88, 91, 97, 100, 121
   defense, 61–62, 67, 99, 118
   growth of Ramo-Wooldridge Company in, 67–68
   growth of TRW in, 80, 88,
   Thompson Products beginnings in, 61–62
El Segundo R&D facility, 74–75, 77
Employee communications, 41, 43–44, 46–47
Employee relations, [human resources], 33, 45, 47, 99
Employees
   African-American, 54–55
   Thompson Products Pledge to, 56
   women, 5, 45, 54, 88
Energy business, 100, 103
Energy Department, 105
Engine Components Group of TRW, 106
Engine valves, automotive *See also* Valves
European Union, 115
Explorer programs, 72–73, 77

F-16 fighter, 100
Falcon guided missile system, 62
Fasteners, 82, 109
Federal Aviation Administration, 105
Federal Motor Vehicle Safety Standard, 109
Fingerprint identification systems, 114–115
Firestone seat belt business, 109
Fleet Satellite Communications System (FLTSATCOM), 91
Flyer's Friend ads, 29
Forbes, 103
Force XXI Battle Command Brigade & Below (FBCB2), 118
Ford, 15, 27, 37, 109. *See also* Big Three automakers
Ford, Henry, 9, 13, 18, 44
Forged engine valves, 15, 17
Fortune, 29, 31, 34, 61, 81, 88
Fortune 500 companies, 80, 102
Foster, John S., 97
Franklin Institute, 9
Friendly Forum, 46–47
Fuel booster pumps, 53

Gallium arsenide technology, 105, 121, 123
Gamma Ray Observatory, 99, 101, 118
General Dynamics, 105
General Electric, 54, 59, 117
General Electronics Group, 67
General Motors (GM), 13, 15, 27, 50, 53–54, 59, 109, 121. *See also* Big Three automakers
George, Harold, 61
Gorman, Joseph (Joe) T., 94–95, 97, 112, 121
   on future of TRW, 122
   in restructuring TRW, 100, 103, 106, 109, 111, 115, 117
Graham, Matt, 33
Grant Ball Company, 7
Great Depression, 31, 33–34, 37–38, 49, 56, 88, 97
Great Observatories, 118
   Chandra X-ray Observatory, 118
   Compton Gamma Ray Observatory, 99, 101, 118
   Hubble Space Telescope, 100
Groocock, John, 97
Guided Missile Research Division, 64, 67. *See also* Space Technology Laboratories

Haise, Fred, 92
Harvard Business School, 85, 100
Heron, Sam D., 20
High Energy Astronomy Observatory program, 91. *See also* Great Observatories
High-speed integrated circuitry, 99–100, 105
Hispano-Suiza V8 engines, 17
Hittite Microwave, 105
Honeywell, 105
Hoover, Herbert, 20
Hopkins, Gloria (Mrs. Charles Thompson), 27
Hubbell, Charles, 27
Hubble Space Telescope, 100
Hughes, Howard, 61
Hughes Aircraft, 61–62, 64
Hughes Tool Company, 61

Imperial Chemical Industries, 109
Indian-tepee logo, 37
Indium phosphide, 121, 123
Industrial and Energy sector of TRW, 100
Industrial Operations Group of TRW, 85
Information Systems of TRW, 105–106
Information technology, 82, 85, 103, 115, 117–118, 121
Inkwell, president's 18–19
Integrated Vehicle Control Systems (IVCS), 117
Intercontinental ballistic missiles (ICBMs). *See* Missile programs
Interior Department, 105
International Land Plane Free-for-All, 25
International TRW businesses, 36–37, 86–88, 91, 93, 112, 115
Internationale Automobil-Ausstellung (AA), 107
Interstellar postcard, 98
Inventory management, 115
Investment Banking, 42
Irving, Jack, 74

Jadson Motor Products Company, 34, 37
Japanese automakers, 99, 109
Jeep Cherokee, 117
Jet propulsion technology *See* Propulsion
Joint Council, 44

Joint ventures of TRW, 80, 87, 109, 118, 121. *See also* Acquisitions of TRW
Jupiter, 64, 98

Kerwin, John, 20
Kingford-Smith, Sir Charles, 24
Knicely, Howard V., 99
Knudsen, William S., 50
Korean War, 49, 59–60, 88
Krider, J. Albert (Pete), 12, 15, 27
Kurtz, David J., 7, 9

Labor relations, effects of Thompson Products management on, 41, 43–45, 47, 54, 56
Labor unions, 41, 44, 47, 54, 56
Lamps, ship, 111
Lasers, 99, 105, 118, 122–123
Let's Have the Truth, 53
Liberty Media Group, 118
Life, 29
Light bulb poster, 103
Lindbergh, Charles, 22–25, 38
Little Brown Hen, 7, 10
Livingstone, Raymond (Ray) S., 22, 33, 47, 49, 54, 56–57, 59, 82, 99
Lockheed Martin, 118
Lovell, Jim, 92
Lucas Aerospace, 118
Lucas lamps, 111
LucasVarity plc., 111, 115, 117–118, 121
Ludlum Steel Company, 17
Lunar excursion module descent engine (LEMDE), 71, 79, 90–92
Lyndhurst headquarters, 97, 99, 103

MST Automotive GmbH Automobile-Sicherheitstechnik, 112
MacArthur, Douglas, 49
Magna International, 112, 117
Management-Labor Policy Committee, 54
Management philosophy, 94
Manhattan Project, 62
Manned Space Flight Program, 77
Marlin-Rockwell Corporation, 80
Martin Marietta, 80
Mass production, 13
Mathews, Samuel M., 7
McBride, Eugene, 33
McCook Field, 20

McDonnell-Douglas, 91

Mettler, Ruben (Rube) F.
in aerospace developments, 72, 74–75, 77–79, 82, 85
as engineer at Ramo-Wooldridge, 64
as president of TRW, 88, 93–95, 97, 105
restructuring of, 100, 103,

Microelectronics, 105

Microwave technology, 105

Miller, Charles L., 109

Millikan, Clark, 74

Millikan Committee, 74

Milstar communication satellite program, 99, 105

Minorities, World War II workforce of, 54–55. See also Women; African-Americans

Minuteman program, 67, 72–73

Missile programs
developed with Ramo-Wooldridge, 62, 64–65, 67
developed with TRW, 72–74, 77, 80, 82, 85, 88, 99, 105,112, 118, 123. See also Aerospace technology

Model T cars, 13, 44, 50

Modules and systems, 109, 117

Morley, John E., 7

Motorola, 99

Mueller, George, 77

National Aeronautic Association, 25

National Aeronautics and Space Administration (NASA), 77, 79, 91
Chandra X-ray Observatory of, 118
Gamma Ray Observatory of, 99, 101, 118
High Energy Astronomy of, 91
Hubble Space Telescope of, 100
Lunar Excursion Module Descent Engine of, 71, 79, 90–92
Orbiting Geophysical Observatory of, 79, 88

National Air Races, 24–25, 38

National Association of Manufacturers (NAM), 54

National Aviation Hall of Fame, 31

National Business Hall of Fame, 31

National Industrial Recovery Act, 41

National Labor Relations Act (1935), 47

National Labor Relations Board (NLRB), 56

National Recovery Administration (NRA), 41

Navy, 91, 105

New Deal, 41, 44, 50

Nielsen, Bud, 74

Norton Air Force Base, 77

Observatory programs
Chandra X-ray, 118
Compton Gamma Ray, 99, 101, 118
High Energy Astronomy, 91
Orbiting Geophysical, 79, 88

Occupant Restraints & Controls Group of TRW, 106

Occupant safety systems
See Automotive safety systems; Air bags; Seat belts; Steering wheels

Old Guard, 44–45

One-in-five meetings, 43

Orbiting Geophysical Observatory (OGO), 79, 88

Orbiting Maneuvering Vehicle, 105

Original equipment, automotive, 33–34, 36, 38, 87

Pace, Stanley (Stan) C., 80, 94, 97, 100

Pacific Semiconductor, 67, 80

Paragon called TRW, A, 103

Passive restraint systems, 108–109

Peacekeeper MX ICBMs, 99

Pearl Harbor, 53, 59, 79

Pentagon, 91. See also Defense Department

Perkins, Frances, 47

Pioneer programs, 67, 72, 77, 88, 91, 98

Pistons, 7, 34

Pledge to employees, 56

Popular Science, 118

Porter, Michael, 100

Pratt & Whitney, 22

President's inkwell, 18–19

Printed circuit boards, 105

Productivity, 97

Program management, 85

Propulsion, 53, 62, 72, 79

Quality, 97

Rack and pinion steering, 87, 91, 99

Ramo, Simon (Si)
in developing missile programs, 64, 67
in developing TRW technologic vision, 80, 85, 105, 115
education and background of, 61–63
role in merging with Thompson Products, 68, 71, 77, 82, 111–112

Ramo-Wooldridge (R-W) Corporation
creation and developments of, 62–65, 67–68, 73, 79–81, 88
incorporated into TRW, 67–69, 122

RAND Corporation, 74

Reagan, Ronald, 88, 97, 99

Reconstruction Finance Corporation, 50

Reda Pump, 100

Redondo Beach Space Center, 77
See also Space Park

Repa Feinstanzwerk, 91, 99, 103, 109

Replacement business, automotive, 20, 33–34, 36–38, 59, 80, 87

Research centers, 112, 117

Restructuring, 103, 105–106, 112, 118, 122

RF Micro Devices, 121

Rich Steel Products, 22, 24

Rich Tool Company, 15, 17

Riley, Edward (Ed) P., 80, 85, 87

Roosevelt, Eleanor, 41

Roosevelt, Franklin D., 41, 44, 50, 54

Ross Gear and Tool Company, 80

Rotocap, 34

Sagan, Carl, 98

Satellites, communication (SCORE/FLTSAT), 72, 91, 99, 105

Satellite technology, 122–123
Astrolink, 118, 121
Defense Support Program, 105
Explorer programs, 72–73
Fleet Satellite Communications, 91
Milstar, 99, 105
Observatories, 79, 88, 99, 101, 118
Orbiting Geophysical Observatory, 79, 88
Pioneer programs, 67, 72, 77, 88, 91, 98
product publicity, 79
Sputnik, 64–65, 67, 72
Tracking and Data Relay, 99
Viking, 88, 91
See also Missile programs

Schriever, Bernhard, 64

SCORE (Signal Communication by Orbiting Relay Equipment), 72

Seat belts, 94, 99, 103, 109, 112
See also Automotive safety systems

Securities and Exchange Commission, 115

Semiconductors, 123

Service Division of Thompson Products, 33, 36–37

Service Packages, 37

Shafts, 54

Shepard, Horace (Shep) A., 61, 71, 78
background of, 53, 59
in diversifying TRW, 62, 79–80, 82, 87–88, 94

Silcrome valves, 17–18, 20, 34

Sinz, Walter A., 24

Site Defense program, 91

6th Circuit Court of Appeals, 56

Smart weaponry, 99, 118

Society of Automotive Engineers (SAE), 27

Sodium-cooled valves, 22, 50, 53

Software, 100, 105

Space & Defense Sector of TRW, 105

Space & Electronics Group of TRW, 106, 118

Space simulator, 77

Spaceborne propulsion systems, 79
See also Propulsion

Spacecraft, 82, 85, 98–99, 105, 118

Space Park, 74–75, 77, 79, 88, 92, 97, 99, 105–106, 112

Space shuttles, 99, 118

Space technology, 105. See also Aerospace technology; Missile programs

Space Technology Laboratories (STL), 67, 82, 85, 88
building of Space Park for, 74–75, 77, 79
functions of, 72–74

Spad fighter planes, 17

Spirit of St. Louis, 22, 24–25

Sputnik, 64–65, 67, 72

Square Deal, 41

Star Wars, 99

Stauffer, George, 33

Steel Products Company, 14, 41
　Fred Crawford at, 17–18
　manufacturing of aircraft valves at, 17
　manufacturing of auto engine valves at, 10, 14–15, 18, 20
　See also Electric Welding Products Company

Steering and suspension components, 15, 27, 59, 86–87, 91, 99, 106, 112, 115, 117

Steering Systems of TRW, 106

Steering wheels, 112. See also Automotive safety systems

Stock
　of Thompson Products, 31, 34, 67
　of TRW, 91, 93

Strategic Defense Initiative (Star Wars), 99

Streetcars, 79. See also Orbiting Geophysical Observatory

Surveyor mooncraft, 79

Swigert, Jack, 92

Switches, 82

Systems & Information Technology Group of TRW, 114, 118

Systems approach, 82, 109, 112, 121

Systems engineering and integration, 61, 64, 74, 82, 85, 115

Systems Group of TRW, 85

Systems Integration Group of TRW, 105

Syvertsen, Jim, 36–37

TRW
　creation of, 68–69, 71, 81–82
　future of, 111, 121–123
　world headquarters of, 97, 99, 103
　roots of, 5

TRW and the 80s, 94

Talley, 109

Tapco, 72, 80, 88
　development and purpose of, 49–50, 53–54
　post-World War II purchase and growth of, 59

Technar, 109

Technology bank, 121

Telecom Italia, 118

Telecommunication systems, 105, 118, 121

Temic Bayern-Chemie Airbag GmbH, 112

Thiokol Corporation, 79

Thompson, Charles (Charlie) E., 59, 64, 82
　beginnings at Cleveland Cap Screw, 10–11
　in manufacturing auto and aircraft valves, 22–23, 25–26, 34, 37
　personal and business qualities of, 25, 27, 29, 33
　as president of Steel Products Co., 14–15, 17–20
　at Electric Welding Products Co., 12–13, 15

Thompson Aircraft Products Company. See Tapco

Thompson Creed, 54

Thompson Products (TP), Inc., 81, 97, 99, 106
　creation of, 10, 15, 20
　Fred Crawford as leader of, 31, 33–34
　Indian tepee logo of, 37
　investment in Ramo-Wooldridge Corporation, 62–64, 67–68, 81
　management and labor at, 43–47, 54–57
　in manufacturing aircraft valves, 22, 24–25, 29
　in manufacturing auto engine valves, 27, 29
　1930s stock prices of, 31, 34
　post-Depression aircraft business of, 33–34, 38
　post-Depression valves and components of, 34
　post-World War II boom at, 56, 59–60
　replacement auto parts business of, 36–38
　World War II developments at, 49–50, 56, 59
　See also Electric Welding Products Company; Steel Products Company

Thompson Products, Ltd., 80

Thompson Products Employees' Association (TPEA), 44

Thompson Products pledge to employees, 56

Thompson Ramo Wooldridge Inc. See TRW

Thompson Trophy, 24–27, 38–39

Thompson Trophy Race, 24, 27, 39

Thomson Electric Welding Company, 7, 10

Thor missiles, 64–65, 67, 72

Time, 54, 67–68

Titan missiles, 64, 67

Tokai Cold Forming Company, 87

Toledo Steel Products Company (TSP), 37

Tools, hand, 82, 100

Tools, industrial, 82, 100

Tracking and Data Relay Satellites, 99

Training programs for employees and supervisors, 47

Transportation Department, 108–109

Treasury Department, 105

"Triangle of Industry and the Production of Wealth," 42

Triangle of Plenty, 18, 42, 44

Turbine blades, wheels, 54, 59

Turbojet engine, 59–60, 67. See also Propulsion

Turner, Roscoe, 38–39

Turner-Laird Special, 39

"Two Wings in Space," 81

Union Club, 10–11

United Auto Workers (UAW), 56

United-Carr, 82, 109

United-Greenfield, 82

Urban League of Cleveland, 55

U.S. Government. See names of specific government departments, armed services, and programs

Valves
　aircraft engine, pre-World War II, 17, 20, 22, 24, 27–29, 37–38
　aircraft, World War II, 50, 53
　automotive engine, 5, 8–12, 14–15, 20, 27, 29, 34, 37, 80, 82, 87, 106, 122
　chromium steel, 17
　engine, 59
　forged, 15, 17
　poppet, 10
　pressure release, 109
　rotating, 34
　silcrome, 17–18, 20, 34
　tungsten steel, 17
　two-piece welded, 15

Van Allen radiation belts, 73

Varity Corp., 111

Vehicle Development Laboratory, 77

Vehicle Dynamics Control Systems, 107

Vela Hotel, 79

VHSIC (very high-speed integrated circuitry), 99–100, 105

Vietnam War, 88

Viking interplanetary probes, 88, 91

Volkswagen, 86–87, 91

Wagner Act (1935), 47, 56

War Advisory Council of Businessmen, 54

War Manpower Commission, 54

Warehouse management, 115

Weapon System Q
See Minuteman program

Webb, J. Sidney (Sid), 80, 82, 88

Weeks, Sinclair, 109

Welding, electric resistance, 7, 10, 12, 15,

Winton, Alexander, 8–10, 15

Winton Motor Carriage Company, 8–9

Wireless communications, 105, 118, 121, 123

Women
　in clean room of Space Park, 88
　as members of Old Guard, 45
　in TRW workforce, 5, 29
　in workforce during World War II, 54

Wooldridge, Dean, 61–64, 67–68, 71, 79, 82, 111–112, 115

World War I, 12, 14–15, 20, 29, 56

World War II, 31, 44, 54, 100
　development of Tapco Plant during, 49–50, 56, 59
　employment of women and minorities during, 54–55

Wright Aeronautical, 17, 22

Wright, J. David (Dave), 33, 50, 53–54, 57, 78, 94
　in creating TRW, 67–68, 71
　in diversifying TRW, 77, 79–80, 88
　as leader of Thompson Products, 59, 61
　three secrets of success, 59

Wright, Orville, 24

Wright Whirlwind engine, 22

Year 2000 U.S. Census, 121

Index of illustrations

Advanced Car Technology Systems center, 116

Advertising, 6, 16, 22, 28, 35, 37, 38, 54, 82-83, 90, 96, 102, 111

Airborne laser, 122

Aircraft components, 60-61

Apollo 13 astronauts, 92

Apollo 13 astronauts, letter from, 93

Articles of Incorporation, 6

Automobiles, early, 8, 13, 21

Bartlett, William, D., 12

Bayles, Lowell, 26

Braking systems, anti-lock, 121

Business Week, 54, 84

Chandra, 119

Circuit boards, 105

Clarkwood plant, 7, 11

Clegg, Lee, 56

Cleveland Plain Dealer, 67

Colwell, Arch, 56

Commercial steering, 80

Compton Gamma Ray Observatory, 101

Coolidge, Jim, 57

Cote, David M., 120

Crawford, Frederick Coolidge, 18, 30, 32, 40, 43, 48, 50, 53–54, 56

Credit reporting, 106

Digitized battlefield, 118

E Award, 50

Ehrenreich & Cie., 86

Electric Welding Products Company employees, 9

Employee communications, 41, 43–44, 46–47, 53, 57

Explorer 6, 73

Fasteners, 109

Fingerprint identification, 114

FLTSATCOM, 91

Forbes, 103

Ford Mustang, 87

Fortune, 81

Friendly Forum, 46–47

Gorman, Joseph T., 95, 110, 111

Headquarters, TRW, 97

Hubbell drawing, 26

Hubbell, Charles H., 27

Indium phosphide, 123

Inkwell, president's, 19

Internationale Automobil-Ausstellung, 107

Interstellar postcard, 98

Krider, J. Albert, 12

Light bulb poster, 102

Lindbergh, Charles, 23, 24

Little Brown Hen, 7, 11

Livingstone, Raymond, 56

Logos, 37, 52, 62, 69, 74, 115

LucasVarity press conference, 111

LucasVarity, 121

Lunar excursion module descent engine, 90

MacArthur, General Douglas, 48–49

Magna/TRW joint venture, 112–113, 116

Mettler, Ruben, F., 74, 77, 84, 88, 95

Milstar, 104

Minorities in the workforce, 55

Minuteman, 73

Moon landing, 70

New York Times, 23

Occupant Safety Systems, 94, 108, 112–113

Old Guard, 45

Orbiting Geophysical Observatory, 78

Pioneer 10, 98

Pledge to employees, 57

Product publicity, 6, 79

Ramo, Simon, 61, 63–64, 66, 70, 84

Reagan, Ronald, 88

Reda pump, 100

Replacement parts, automotive, 36

Rollover test, 116

Schriever, Bernhard, 64

Shepard, Horace A., 53, 59, 70, 78, 84

Solar Power Conversion System, 81

Space Park employees, 77, 89

Space Park, 74–75

Space simulator, 76

Space Technology Laboratories employees, 72

Spad fighter plane, 17

Steering systems, 86, 99

Stock certificates, 31, 69

Tapco, 51–52, 58, 60

Telegram, Lindbergh flight, 22

Thompson, Charles, E., 10, 26

Thompson Trophy, 25–26

Thor missile, 65

Time, 66

Tracking and Data Relay Satellite, 99

Triangle of Plenty, 42

Turner, Roscoe, 39

Union Club, Cleveland, 11

Valve manufacturing, 4, 8, 11, 15, 16, 29

Winton, Alexander, 8

Women in the workforce, 4, 29, 55, 89

Wooldridge, Dean, 61, 63, 66

World War I, parade during, 14

Wright, J. David, 53, 57–58, 68, 70, 84

Reproductions on the following pages are part of the TRW collection, housed at the Western Reserve Historical Society, Cleveland, Ohio:
4, 6, 8, 11–12, 16, 18, 22–23, 26–27, 32, 38–41, 44–46, 50–54, 57–58, 60–61, 70, 81, 84.

Inside back cover:
FLTSATCOM.
See page 91.

www.ingramcontent.com/pod-product-compliance
Lightning Source LLC
Chambersburg PA
CBHW042128100426
42812CB00017B/2646